INDONESIAN SEA NOMADS

The Orang Suku Laut consider themselves indigenous Malays. Yet their interaction with others who call themselves Malays is characterised on both sides by fear of harmful magic and witchcraft. The nomadic Orang Suku Laut believe that the Qur'an contains elements of black magic, while the settled Malays consider the nomads dangerous, dirty and backward. At the centre of this study, based on first hand anthropological data, is the symbolism of money and the powerful influence it has on social relationships within the Riau archipelago.

The first major publication on these maritime nomadic communities, the book adds fresh perspectives to anthropological debates on exchange systems, tribality, and hierarchy. It also characterises the different ways of being Malay in the region and challenges the prevailing tendency to equate Malay identity with the Islamic faith.

Cynthia Chou is Associate Professor of Southeast Asian Studies at the University of Copenhagen.

RoutledgeCurzon-IIAS Asian Studies Series

Series Co-ordinator: Dick van der Meij
Institute Director: Wim A.L. Stokhof

The International Institute for Asian Studies (IIAS) is a postdoctoral research centre based in Leiden and Amsterdam, The Netherlands. Its main objective is to encourage Asian Studies in the Humanities and the Social Sciences and to promote national and international co-operation in these fields. The Institute was established in 1993 on the initiative of the Royal Netherlands Academy of Arts and Sciences, Leiden University, Universiteit van Amsterdam and Vrije Universiteit Amsterdam. It is mainly financed by The Netherlands Ministry of Education, Culture, and Sciences. IIAS has played an active role in co-ordinating and disseminating information on Asian Studies throughout the world. The Institute acts as an international mediator, bringing together various entities for the enhancement of Asian Studies both within and outside The Netherlands. The RoutledgeCurzon-IIAS Asian Studies series reflects the scope of the Institute. The Editorial Board consists of Erik Zürcher, Wang Gungwu, Om Prakash, Dru Gladney, Amiya K. Bagchi, James C. Scott, Jean-Luc Domenach and Frits Staal.

Images of the 'Modern Woman' in Asia
Edited by Shoma Munshi

Nomads in the Sedentary World
Edited by Anatoly M. Khazanov & Andre Wink

Reading Asia
Edited by Frans Husken & Dick van der Meij

Tourism, Heritage and National Culture in Java
Heidi Dahles

Asian-European Perspectives
Edited by Wim Stokhof & Paul van der Velde

Law and Development in East and Southeast Asia
Edited by Christoph Antons

The Indian Ocean Rim
Edited by Gwyn Campbell

Rethinking Chinese Transnational Enterprises
Edited by Leo Douw, Cen Huang & David Ip

'Hinduism' in Modern Indonesia
Edited by Martin Ramstedt

Indonesian Sea Nomads
Cynthia Chou

Diasporas and Interculturalism in Asian Performing Arts
Edited by Hae-Kyung Um

Reading East Asian Writing
Edited by Michel Hockx & Ivo Smits

INDONESIAN SEA NOMADS

MONEY, MAGIC, AND FEAR OF THE ORANG SUKU LAUT

Cynthia Chou

RoutledgeCurzon
Taylor & Francis Group
LONDON AND NEW YORK

First published 2003
by RoutledgeCurzon, an imprint of Taylor & Francis
11 New Fetter Lane, London EC4P 4EE

Simultaneously published in the USA and Canada
by RoutledgeCurzon
29 West 35th Street, New York, NY 10001

RoutledgeCurzon is an imprint of the Taylor & Francis Group

© 2003 Cynthia Chou

Typeset in Times New Roman by Dick van der Meij
Printed and bound in Great Britain by St Edmundbury Press,
Bury St Edmunds, Suffolk

All rights reserved. No part of this book may be reprinted or reproduced or utilised in any form or by any electronic, mechanical, or other means, now known or hereafter invented, including photocopying and recording, or in any information storage or retrieval system, without permission in writing from the publishers.

The publisher makes no representation, express or implied, with regard to the accuracy of the information contained in this book and cannot accept any legal responsibility or liability for any errors or omissions that may be made.

British Library Cataloguing in Publication Data
A catalogue record for this book is available from the British Library

Library of Congress Cataloging in Publication Data
Chou, Cynthia, 1963-
Indonesian Sea Nomads: money, magic, and fear of the Orang Suku Laut /
Cynthia Chou.
p. cm. – (RoutledgeCurzon-IIAS studies series)
1. Bajau (Southeast Asian people)–Ethnic identity. 2. Bajau (Southeast Asian people)–Economic conditions. 3. Bajau (Southeast Asian people)–Psychology. 4. Ethnopsychology–Indonesia–Riau (Province) 5. Money–Social aspects–Indonesia–Riau (Province) 6. Muslims–Indonesia–Riau (Province) 7. Riau (Indonesia): Province–Social life and customs.
I. Title. II. Series.
DS632.B24 C56 2002
306.3'4'0899928–dc21
2002068161

ISBN 0-700-1724-2

For my James

Contents

Acknowledgements   x
Map   xii

1. Money, Magic, and Fear of the Orang Suku Laut   1
2. The Setting   15
3. Ranking in Riau   24
4. *Ilmu*   52
5. The Meaning of Things: Constructions of the Orang Laut's Identity   73
6. Sharing and Helping: Constructions of the Orang Laut's Identity   85
7. Money: Reconstructing the Meaning of Things   108
8. Reflections and Challenges   141

Glossary   145
References   149

ACKNOWLEDGEMENTS

In preparing the first version of this book, I benefited greatly from the criticism and advice of Doctors Leo Howe, Stephen Hugh-Jones, Keith Hart of the University of Cambridge, and Dr. Janet Carsten of the University of Edinburgh. Special mention has to be made of Dr. Vivienne Wee of the City University of Hong Kong and Dr. Geoffrey Benjamin of Nanyang Technological University for first suggesting the Orang Suku Laut as my subject of field research, and for the stimulating exchange of ideas for all these many years. The earlier stage of my research, including many trips to the field, was supported by generous awards from the British Council, the J.E. Cairnes Scholarship from Girton College, University of Cambridge, and the Crowther-Benyon Fund from the Museum of Archaeology and Anthropology, University of Cambridge. Updating and rewriting were done during my tenure at the International Institute for Asian Studies, Leiden; and the Department of Asian Studies, University of Copenhagen, kindly freed me from my teaching duties for a semester to work on the final draft of this book. I have Dr. Lloyd Haft of the University of Leiden to thank for the final shape of the book: he taught me how to arrange my ideas for clearer presentation.

The Indonesian Government kindly granted me permission to do fieldwork in remote areas of the country, which was then made possible to realize by efforts and assistance from numerous scholars and officials from *Lembaga Ilmu Pengetahuan* (the Indonesian Institute of Sciences in Jakarta), the Universitas Pekanbaru in Riau, and other offices in Pekanbaru, Riau, and Batam.

My heartfelt gratitude goes to all my Orang Suku Laut, Malay, and Chinese friends for the care and trust they accorded me throughout my fieldwork among them. In particular, I thank Mr. Cou Acuk, Mrs. Cou Su Lang, and Mr. Cou Ahua of Pulau Sembur for their generous hospitality. Kakak Pindah, Mrs. Lai Tee and their families were never hesitant in extending a welcome to me. My *mamak angkat* Suri, her husband Tekong, and their family treated me as their own during my time in Pulau Nanga. There was always room for me in their *sampan*. I thank Halus and Baggong for their delightful company and for teaching me how not to row backwards. Across in Teluk Nipah, Meen and his family accepted me into their home. Further off in Pulau Abang, Asim and his family fed and sheltered me. In Dapur Enma, Awang Ketah, Ibu Saya, and their family met every need I had. Atong and his family allowed me into their midst while I was in Tiang Wang Kang. In Pulau Penyengat, the late Raja Hamzah Yunus, whom I shall miss sorely, and my *bapak angkat* Raja Haji Abdul Rahim Mansor and their wives received me and visitors of mine with graciousness and gave exceptional guidance on the history of Riau. In Tanjung Pinang, Mr. Cou Ngouti and his family opened their home to me. In Pekanbaru, I met Abang Jufri Gafar who out of concern for a woman fieldworker alone insisted upon introducing me to his family in Tanjung Pinang. It is with much sadness that I recall his late mother, Ibu Rahmah Yahya, for her kindness and joviality in giving me a home away from home. Nenenda Zauyah, Tri Kurniati, the late Farah, and Abang Muryono were the rest who made up this wonderful family.

I thank Eric Liang for rescuing me from my endless and often self-generated computer-related problems in preparing this book. Faye Chan provided publications that were difficult to obtain. Dick van der Meij, my editor at the International Institute of Asian Studies, Leiden, saw to it that the book has the most appealing appearance.

It remains for me to thank my family. Back in the olden days it was my sister Cindy who first brought my attention to the possibility of obtaining a British Council scholarship in support of my research ambition. My mother has given support and understanding ever since in spite of the fact that she would thus have an absentee daughter. Last of all I acknowledge the affectionate support of James, which I expect to receive for many more volumes to come.

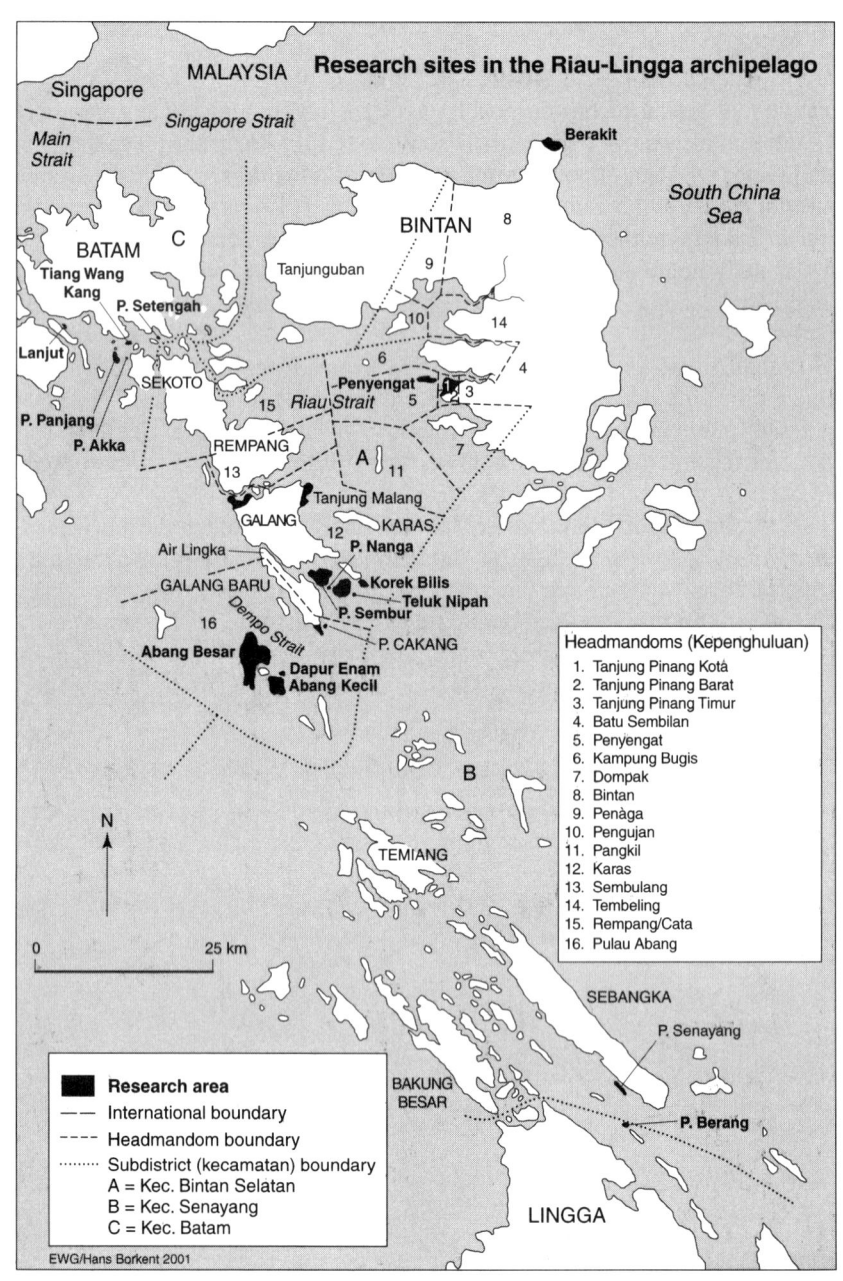

Map 1. Research sites in the Riau-Lingga archipelago

Chapter 1

Money, Magic, and Fear of the Orang Suku Laut

Picture 1: An Orang Laut *sampan*: home and work place

This book is about the symbolism of money and the profound power it exerts in transforming the Orang Suku Laut's identity in the Riau Archipelago of Indonesia. Indonesians often refer to the Orang Suku Laut as 'orang laut' (sea people) and 'suku sampan' (boat tribe). In current literature, they are variously known as 'sea nomads,' 'sea folk' (Sopher, 1977:47), 'sea hunters and gatherers' (*ibid*:218), 'sea gypsies' (Thomson, 1851:140), and 'people of the sea' (Sandbukt, 1982). In this book, I use the shorter term 'Orang Laut.' It has been reported that in Malay, the term 'Orang Laut' refers not only to sea nomads but also to 'ordinary' coastal-dwelling Malays who are engaged in maritime occupations (see for example Lenhart, 1997; Sather, 1998:21). Lenhart (quoted from Sather, 1998:35) also reports that in Riau, the tribal indigenes prefer to be called Orang Suku Laut, rather than Orang Laut. I do not dispute Lenhart's findings or Sather's (1998) argument. My decision to use the term 'Orang Laut' rests upon my fieldwork experiences in which I found my tribal friends and other Indonesians preferring the briefer term 'Orang Laut' in their daily conversations.

As tribal indigenes of the Riau Archipelago in Indonesia, the Orang Laut are also generally recognized as the indigenous Malays of Riau. Yet in the interaction between the Malays and the Orang Laut, there exists much fear and suspicion with constant accusations of being poisoned and harmed by each other through practices of magic and witchcraft. This stems from the Malays' perception of the Orang Laut as a 'dangerous, dirty and unprogressive people.' To the Malays, the Orang Laut are a people who prefer a life of nomadism which is deemed unconducive to adhering to the Islamic faith. On the other hand, the Orang Laut regard the Muslim Malays with equal suspicion as they believe that the Qur'an contains elements of black magic teachings.

In this book, I explore how perceptions of self-and-other have shaped the image of the Orang Laut and the Malays, and have become enmeshed in the dynamics of social interaction in their exchange economy. This is of great consequence as the perception of who the Orang Laut are directly affects who can exchange with whom, which items can be safely exchanged without fear of dire consequences, and how these exchanges can take place in acceptably safe terms between the transactors. Money, as I will show, holds the symbolic power in the Riau Archipelago to affect the nature of these social relationships. In connection with this, I will also explore the meaning and moral implications of monetary and commercial exchanges in contrast to exchanges of other kinds that take place between the Orang Laut and other Malay and non-Malay communities in the region.

The Spirit that Resides in Things and People

There is a direct relationship between material things and group identities among the Orang Laut and Malays. Both groups classify artefacts and skills into categories to reinforce their material expression and intersubjective order for patterns of interaction within the Malay World. These artefacts and skills have become positional markers for members in the Malay World to signify their relatedness or difference. As such, the choice or avoidance of such things and skills is interpreted as conveying affiliation or non-affiliation with a sub-culture.

A complex of things exists within Orang Laut communities. They range from items with inherent meanings and values to those whose meanings and values undergo redefinition as they circulate through different domains of exchange within and beyond Orang Laut communities. My aim is to locate the analysis of these things within the broader spectrum of the perceived social order of what it means to be an Orang Laut or a Malay in Riau.

Mauss's (1990) theory of the gift revolves around the spirit that is embedded in persons and things. This spirit is the axis around which the obligations to give, accept, and reciprocate converge. Aspects of Mauss's idea of the spirit that resides in things and people can be extended to looking at the patterns of exchange, group relations and identity between the Orang Laut and Malays. Mauss's view has been widely debated by Levi-Strauss (1987), Firth (1959), Sahlins (1974), and Parry (1986), just to name a few. Levi-Strauss (1987) has argued for the need to look beyond reasons for the metaphysical aspect of things to the deeper reality of the structural features of exchange. He (*ibid*:46) proposes that the 'whole theory calls for the existence of a structure' which views things as a totality. Refuting Mauss's theory, Firth (1959) has also stressed the importance of examining the economic ethics of the thing, rather than the spirit of the person that enforces reciprocity in gift giving (see also Malinowski, 1922; 1966). Later, Sahlins (1974) attempted to synthesize Mauss's ideas with those of Levi-Strauss and Firth. He has looked at both the underlying structures and the practical reasons for exchange. He agrees with Mauss that gift exchange is an analogy of the social and political contract, facilitating the peace that in civil society is secured by the state. However, he disagrees with Mauss's idea of the importance of understanding the spiritual essence of the donor in explaining gift exchange. Parry (1986:456), in his analysis of the Indian gift, defends Mauss's notion of the 'spirit of the gift,' but argues with Mauss's notion of the ethic of reciprocity in gift exchange. He demonstrates the idea of unilateral exchanges in the Indian gift. This is because an Indian gift embodies the sins of the donor and is given to the Brahmin priests without the slightest desire for reciprocity. While I can see the plausibility of the arguments by Levi-Strauss, Firth and Sahlins in the data that I have collected, and have applied them in some instances to my analysis of the exchange of things within Orang Laut communities, I have at the same time found it impossible to refute Mauss's theory on the metaphysical aspect of things in its entirety. I join the debate regarding Mauss's theory of the gift by proposing that it is necessary to look beyond the generality of things to the particularity of things in relation to their political and historical contexts (see also Thomas, 1991:18). This, coupled with an understanding of the supernatural aspects of things within Orang Laut communities, will explain the fears and expectations surrounding the acts of giving, accepting, and reciprocating, and why gifts are rejected by those from other groups of Orang Laut and non-Orang Laut communities.

There are a number of things within Orang Laut communities which are thought to embody inherent supernatural powers. These powers are independent of any forms of exchange which might affect their inalienable value (Weiner, 1985). This supernatural aspect also accounts for the indissoluble bond between certain things and their owners. Not surprisingly, these things cannot be given away or circulated between different communities. On the other hand, there are things within the Orang Laut communities which have social value created or enhanced in them through different forms of exchange. They embody less supernatural powers. Therefore, it is the belief in the spirit that resides in things and people which explains why others attempt to distance themselves from certain types of things originating in an Orang Laut territory. From the perspective of the Orang Laut and their non-Orang Laut transactors, things are differentiated by their degrees of supernatural power. Boundaries have been set up to determine the respective forms in which these different types of things may circulate. These boundaries act as barriers to the types of things which may or may not circulate out of Orang Laut territories. They also dictate the different forms of exchange that one should or can engage in with different groups of people. Things can thus be primarily located in a system of social classification which has significant bearing on one's identity within the Malay World.

In all of this, the spirit of the person has merged to a greater or lesser extent with the things he or she possesses. As things therefore bear the same identity as their owners, they relate to the question of being Orang Laut or non-Orang Laut. In this sense, things have become metonymic signs for their owners. In Leach's (1989:33) theory of the logic by which signs and symbols are connected, he states that 'signs and most symbols and signals cohere as sets. Meanings depend on contrast.' When signs or symbols are used to distinguish one class of things or actions from another, artificial boundaries, such as that between pure and impure Malays, are created in a field which is perceived as 'naturally' continuous. It is also the nature of such markers of boundaries to be ambiguous in implication, thus becoming a source of conflict and anxiety. The switching of boundaries or social frontiers for things which are metonymic signs for their owners calls for a ritual. As Leach (*ibid*:33) states, 'the crossing of frontiers and thresholds is always hedged about with ritual, so also is the transition from one social status to another'. In the case of the Orang Laut, I will show that money is used as a vehicle to distance certain types of things from their owners when they circulate out of Orang Laut communities into non-Orang Laut communities.

Here I modify Leach's (1989:40) idea on metaphoric condensations to offer an underlying framework for understanding the system of social classification for the Orang Laut in the Malay World. The following argument shows the metaphoric condensations of things and how they set up symbolic boundaries for the Orang Laut. I suggest that from the point of view of a member of an Orang Laut community, the metaphoric condensations of things in his or her group are roughly as follows.

1. 'We Orang Laut, the indigenous Malays, and other Malays are all members of one social group, the Malay World. This is because we are descended from a common ancestor.' (This is initially an idea in the mind.)
2. Similarly, 'they, the Malays, are all members of one social group. This is because they are descended from a common ancestor.' (This is also initially an idea in the mind.)
3. These things and *ilmu* or services are ours (Orang Laut). Those are the Malays' etc. (These are classificatory statements belonging to the context of non-human nature or the material culture.)
4. That 'we' differ from 'the Malays,' as 'things of the Orang Laut' differ from 'things of the Malays,' is a simple metaphor.
5. 'We' are identified with things of the Orang Laut because our ancestors' identity is embedded in those things. Premise (5) is thus a logical consequence of premises (1) to (4).
6. In adopting the use of money to distance our identity from a thing, and to transform the meaning and social value of things that are circulating out of our territory towards a Malay territory, we and the Malays both are showing reverence to our identity and/or ancestors which are, to a greater or lesser degree, represented in things.

The significance of money has been widely discussed. From Aristotle (1962) to Karl Marx (1961), the impact of money has been passionately debated as an entity deteriorating community and personal identities, as well as dichotomizing the global society into peasants and capitalists. In contrast, Adam Smith (1904) maintained that society's happiness and prosperity are generated by individual pursuit of monetary gain. Between these polarized views have been a myriad intermediate positions. For example, Simmel (1978) has asserted that money is the instrument for expanding trust and human freedom, while warning of its threat to the moral order. These ideological debates, however, fall short of an understanding of the solid foundation on which money stands and the interplay of its forces that is shaping and re-shaping the modern social world including the Malay World in Riau. Parry and Bloch, in their *Money and the Morality of Exchange* (1991), have argued convincingly that whichever position western intellectual thought has taken, money is credited with the intrinsic power to revolutionize society and culture. In the perspective of their documentation and analysis of how diverse world views and various economic systems perceive the use and representation of money, this power is the recognition of the way actors themselves construct money symbolically. Theirs is an important contribution to our understanding of the various ways in which money can be symbolically represented when we juxtapose various cultures in a single time span. It is my interest in this book to take this argument a step further. Money must be seen as part of a secular theology in a global movement merging 'we' and 'they' to establish frameworks of peace in markets and states, enabling people to exchange around the world. I thus attempt to transcend an endogenous cultural logic of understanding how identities are constructed at a regional level and move instead towards looking at the local-global interconnections in constructing or even transforming identities. Most studies on tribal identities have focused on how identities are constructed at the local-regional level. By going beyond these conventions, the connections between intercommunity divisions – regional, national, and global identities – can be better highlighted. As an imaginative construct that can be viewed from different perspectives, the symbolism of money will bring us to the wider cultural negotiations that touch the centre of local affairs.

EXPLORATIONS

I first travelled to the Riau Archipelago in August 1991 and stayed until October 1992. Ever since then, I have been returning to the field annually for periods varying from a few weeks to three months to visit old friends in former field sites as well as to explore new places and establish new contacts. My fieldwork has been and continues to be carried out in an area that had for a long time been considered a peripheral region in Indonesia.

The clusters of island communities that I have studied span across the *Kepenghuluan* (Headmandoms) of Karas, Pulau Abang, Batam, Bintan, Penyengat, and Tanjung Pinang Kota. These Headmandoms are governed by the administrative unit *Kecamatan Bintan Selatan* (Sub-District of Southern Bintan) which is situated in Tanjung Pinang (see Map, p. xii). This Sub-District is in turn governed by the administrative body *Kabupaten Kepulauan Riau* (District of the Riau Archipelago) which also has its administrative centre in Tanjung Pinang. This District is further subsumed under the administrative unit known as *Propinsi Riau* (Riau Province), the capital of which is Pekanbaru on Sumatra.[1] Riau Province is, finally, subordinate to the national capital of Jakarta. There are thus four intervening administrative levels between Jakarta and my field area. In addition, I also carried out fieldwork in the islands of Berang and Senayang in the Sub-District of Senayang.

Prior to my fieldwork, my preconceptions of the Orang Laut were shaped by the type of literature then available to me, and by Indonesian friends who kindly offered me their conceptions of the Orang Laut. These views were what enabled me to contextualize and understand the information which I was later to gather from both my Orang Laut and non-Orang Laut friends.

There has been some ongoing work on the Bajau Laut, a group of Southeast Asian sea nomads.[2] However, recent literature based on field research on the Orang Laut remains dismal.[3] It has been almost fifty years since the older literature, almost all written before the mid-nineteenth century, on the Orang Laut was thoroughly analysed in a doctoral dissertation by David Sopher (1954) which was first published in 1965 and later reprinted with a postscript in 1977. Even then, Sopher's geographical cum historical study of the sea nomads was based entirely on the published research and observations of other writers. Little in-depth study of the Orang Laut has been undertaken since; what we can find are fragmentary discussions in scattered articles or unpublished academic dissertations.[4] Consequently, most of the published literature on the Orang Laut dates from the mid-nineteenth century. It comprises a heterogeneous collection of travel accounts, geographical monographs, local histories and administrative reports.[5] This constituted my main source of information prior to my first fieldtrip in 1991. Such literature presented a picture of a 'lower class of Malays' (Findlayson and Raffles, 1826, in Gibson-Hill 1973:122) who behaved like 'wild animals' (Hill, 1973:97). The Orang Laut were often seen as people who seldom came ashore and who mostly lived in their boats (Hill, 1973:106).

Such views of the Orang Laut were echoed when I first met the Indonesian authorities to secure the necessary official travel documents to commence my fieldwork. Out of concern, the officers and other Indonesians with whom I came into contact tried in every way to dissuade me from interacting with the Orang Laut. They described them as 'smelly people who never bathe,' 'people who do not wear clothes,' 'people who do not have bathrooms,' and 'people who live and do everything in their boats.'[6] Invariably, I was cautioned that I, as someone from another world, was completely ignorant in comparison to the 'people of Indonesia' who know that 'the Orang Laut possess no religion and do not pray at all.' These concerned Indonesians were worried that I would be bewitched and poisoned by the Orang Laut, whom they believed to possess the most powerful form of *ilmu hitam* (black magic). The usual scenario painted for me by my well-wishers was that I would be bewitched into forgetting and abandoning everything about myself and my family ties, and finally marrying an Orang Laut.

Unbeknown to my well-wishers, their 'inside' information only fuelled my curiosity about the Orang Laut. When these acquaintances finally realized that their warnings had only served to produce an effect contrary to their intended meaning, they very reluctantly advised me on issues pertinent to my safety. I was told that I should never facially or verbally express any criticism in front of the Orang Laut, no matter how smelly or dirty they were. I was warned that if they felt insulted, I would be bewitched into marrying one of them. Unfailingly this was followed by the advice that under no circumstance should I ever accept anything offered by an Orang Laut, nor should I give any of my personal belongings to them. This was because I could be bewitched through these things. The most serious offence would be for me to tell the Orang Laut that I did not believe in their magical prowess. I was cautioned that this would either insult or challenge the Orang Laut into bewitching me. I was also left feeling very confused when I was told that I should not address someone as, or even ask if a person was, an Orang Laut. The term 'Orang Laut,' I was taught, carried derogatory and insulting implications.

If my curiosity about the Orang Laut had been aroused, I was also intrigued by my Malay well-wishers in particular. This was because the Malays, while cautioning me about the Orang Laut, did recognize the claims of the Orang Laut to being the *suku Melayu asli* (original Malay divisions) and *orang asli Melayu* (indigenous Malays) of the Malay World, of which Riau is a part.[7] The Malays see the Orang Laut as unprogressive and *jahat* (evil) and take great pride in this perceived distinction, on the basis of which they differentiate themselves: 'people like us would never be able to adapt to that sort of life.'[8]

The way the Orang Laut saw me, talked about me, and treated my presence in their midst also constituted important data in contextualizing not only my own but also their understanding of the dynamics of group boundaries. Therefore, throughout this book, I have not shied away from presenting ethnographic accounts in which I have been the principal participant. I have not changed the names of the people whose lives I discuss. Most of the Orang Laut who shared and continue to share their lives with me wish to be recognized. For the few who have requested anonymity, I have changed their names to protect their privacy.

Due to the general lack of updated information on the Orang Laut, I was at a complete loss when I first embarked on my field explorations to locate the Orang Laut. At that time, I was dependent on the goodwill of two Malay aristocrats bearing the title of 'Raja' from Penyengat Island, who offered to act as my guides. I had by then realized that the Malays were afraid of my desire to associate with the Orang Laut. However, what I was still ignorant of was the extent and intensity of the tensions between the Malays and Orang Laut. I was therefore undiscriminating in my choice of guides, and my association with these Malay aristocrats caused crippling problems in the early stages. My guides were insistent that I live with Malay or Chinese families on nearby Malay islands for the purpose of observing from afar the neighbouring Orang Laut communities. At certain points, almost entire Malay communities orchestrated a collective effort in advising me to stay away from the Orang Laut. The Chinese regarded me as one of them and were just as adamant that I live with them. I was desperate for a solution. I had to be careful not to insult the hospitality of the Malays and the Chinese when I explained my need to be with the Orang Laut. My solution was finally to spend different periods of time living in the Malay, Chinese and Orang Laut communities. This proved a resourceful solution as it situated me in different positions to observe the self-and-other perceptions of each of these communities.

The Orang Laut were initially suspicious of my association with the Malays. However, my earnest struggles to establish close rapport with them and to learn their language soon convinced them that I was different. The first indications of their acceptance of me came in how they interpreted my presence amongst them. They reasoned that although my family home was in Singapore, I was living in Europe and was intending to return to Europe again. They saw that I liked and wanted to stay in Riau, and thus concluded that I was 'like an Orang Laut' moving from place to place. They soon adopted me as a member of their community through the very exchange practices that I was cautioned by my non-Orang Laut informants to avoid lest I be bewitched into following an Orang Laut's way of life.

Generally speaking, the literature on the Malays tends to treat the Orang Laut as a homogenous group. This has arisen because of insufficient historical consideration. Far from being homogenous, they show great diversity in their forms of cultural and social organization.[9] Not only is the literature misleading in this respect; most Malays today also tend to think of them as a homogenous group, only to be found somewhere far off in the Dabo Singkep area of the Archipelago – an area which, I was told, no Malay would ever venture to inhabit. Such claims are significant as they revealed to me where the Malays thought the Orang Laut were concentrated, and contributed to my understanding of the self-and-other perceptions between these two peoples.

The picture of a homogenized Orang Laut community was quickly proven incorrect as I travelled among numerous islands in the first few weeks of my fieldwork to look for a suitable field-site. I discovered very quickly that the Orang Laut consisted of many related and unrelated subgroups. From the start of my field explorations, I was constantly confronted with tensions that existed in the interaction between the Orang Laut and Malays, and to a lesser extent, with the Chinese and other groups. These tensions were also present when different or unrelated groups of Orang Laut interacted. The overt expression of all this, I discovered, was clearly seen in the exchange practices of material objects and services between the different communities.

My early field observations soon made me realize that in studying the Orang Laut, I could not select a single island community. Nor was it feasible to restrict myself to a single Orang Laut clan, even if it were possible to isolate such an entity. I was convinced that, were I to do so, vital observations on inter-group relations would be lost. I decided that my study would not be a village ethnography, but a discussion of the interaction between different groups of Orang Laut and non-Orang Laut scattered throughout the Archipelago. My decision was accordingly to carry out my fieldwork in clusters of island communities throughout the Archipelago.

In the Riau Archipelago that I describe, people often mix vocabulary from various languages and dialects. The combination of *Bahasa Indonesia* and *Bahasa Melayu* is most common. The two languages are closely related linguistically, but the distinctions are politically significant, the former being the national language of the Republic of Indonesia, and the latter the language of a wider Malay World stretching far beyond the Republic. Many Orang Laut are able to converse in both. Each Orang Laut clan also possesses its own dialect. As each clan occupies a different territory, clan members are often able to speak a common dialect of the region in which their territory is situated. Moreover, the Orang Laut's mobility brings them into contact with still other ethnic communities, thus enabling many to become truly multi-lingual. A number of them have even become fluent in the Chinese dialect Teochiu through their dealings with the Teochiu-speaking Chinese middlemen who help them sell their maritime products. During the course of my fieldwork, I found that many Orang Laut were keen to let me know of their multi-lingual ability by mixing vocabularies from the many languages and dialects that they knew. This was to show their vast exposure to and knowledge of the maritime world. The Malays speak a combination of *Bahasa Melayu* and *Bahasa Indonesia* in addition to their respective sub-regional dialects. The Chinese share very much the same linguistic abilities as the Malays in addition to their mastery of various Chinese dialects, of which Teochiu is especially common. A few Chinese also speak Mandarin. I carried out my fieldwork mostly in a mixture of *Bahasa Melayu* and *Bahasa Indonesia*. Although I was able to record certain data that were told to me in *Bahasa Galang*, I was not able to speak it very well. Almost all of my Chinese informants were fluent in *Bahasa Indonesia*, but, for obvious reasons, they were more eager to converse with me in Teochiu and Mandarin. Unless otherwise stated, all my quotations are translated from *Bahasa Indonesia* and *Bahasa Melayu*.

Textual Organization

To fill the glaring gaps in our knowledge of the Orang Laut and generally of *orang asli* (indigenous) populations, I begin with an amplification of ethnographic detail on the Orang Laut. This is intended as a contribution towards our knowledge of the indigenous history of Riau, Singapore and Malaysia, which before present-day political territorial demarcations stood as a single political entity, the Malay World.

In seeking to look at the exchange economy and dynamics of social interaction between the Orang Laut and other Malay and non-Malay communities in Chapter 5 to 7, I examine the identity of the Orang Laut in relation to the social history and the power structure in the Malay World. I concentrate in Chapter 4 on why the Orang Laut are widely feared, especially by the Malays who embrace Islam. What is most feared is that one could be bewitched by the Orang Laut's powerful *ilmu hitam* and subsequently *ikut* (follow) an Orang Laut into the lowest ranks of being Malay. This raises the question: what exactly does being a pure Malay in Riau mean? What does this process towards purity embrace and entail? In this chapter, I also begin an analysis of what are deemed to be the 'impure and evil' black magic practices of the Orang Laut.

These preceding chapters set the background for understanding how the identity of the Orang Laut has been formed and how it affects the dynamics of social interaction in Riau. The bulk of the book continues with an explication of detailed ethnographic accounts of the different levels of interaction and exchange patterns among the Orang Laut themselves, between the different groups of Orang Laut, and between the Orang Laut and the Malays and Chinese. What does it mean to exchange gifts? Why is this form of exchange feared and avoided between different groups in the Malay World? In contrast, how does the exchange of the very same items within a cash economy come to be regarded as safe and acceptable? My concern is to see how aspects of sociality are removed as an item moves from being a gift to being a commodity. What does money mean to the Orang Laut? The use of money has enabled the Malays to interact with, touch, and even obtain magic potions from the Orang Laut with less fear of being poisoned. I will show how money holds the power in Riau to transform symbolically the nature of social relationships. At the same time, I will also examine how social relationships have shaped the use and meaning of money. Chapter 7 looks at the role of the Chinese merchants and middlemen in Riau. To my knowledge, no in-depth study has been carried out on the relationship between these two peoples. The Chinese middlemen play a key role in moving items to and from an Orang Laut community in Riau, and even for export purposes to Singapore and beyond. Rather than being considered *orang dari luar* (people from outside) (Wee, 1985:54), the local born Chinese are referred to as *peranakan*s (people of mixed origins).[10] They are seen as a distinct group who are involved in, but not part of the Malay World. Interestingly, it is through the mediation of this non-indigenous and 'mixed origins' group that items are rendered safer and more acceptable for all peoples in the Malay World. The Malays and the Orang Laut fear to receive things coming directly from each other but, as things pass through the hands of the Chinese middleman, social distance is added to them, thus neutralizing meanings which otherwise would have prohibited a transaction.

The participation of the Orang Laut in a wider exchange economy involving money breaks down certain barriers for them. The use of money has allowed them some interaction with the Malays and other non-Malay communities. However, this also has broader implications for their identity. A new challenge for further research is to examine how market relations have already given or can potentially give redefinitions to indigenous categorizations and meanings of things and skills, leading in turn to the construction of more new identities.

NOTES

1   The history of Pekanbaru is described by Kato (1984:10) as follows:

It initially developed as a riverside market town in the late eighteenth century. During the Dutch period it grew to be an important port town which accommodated steamships relatively deep in the interior of inland Riau. However, Pekanbaru was still a small town of 2,990 souls in 1930. Its fortunes dramatically turned upward when large reserves of oil were found by Caltex near it in 1939; the exploration of these reserves began soon after the Second World War. In 1960, the capital city of the still young Province of Riau was moved from Tanjung Pinang in island Riau to Pekanbaru.

2   There is a dearth of knowledge on the sea nomads of Southeast Asia and of nomadic maritime communities in general. The few relevant major works include *Sea Nomads: A Study Based on the Literature of the Maritime Boat People of Southeast Asia* by David Sopher (1965). In 1960, Hans Kähler wrote *Ethnographische und linguistiche Studien über die Orang Darat, Orang Akit, Orang Laut und Orang Utan im Riau-Archipel und auf den Inseln an der Ostküste von Sumatra*. Another book was *The Moken* by Jacques Ivanoff (1997). Among studies of sea nomads, most works that have been published have concentrated on the Bajau. For example: *The Sea People of Sulu* by H. Arlo Nimmo (1972), *Celebrations with the Sun: An Overview of Religious Phenomena among the Badjaos* by Bruno Bottignolo (1995), and *The Bajau Laut: Adaptation, History, and Fate in a Maritime Fishing Society of South-Eastern Sabah* by Clifford Sather (1997).
3   For more on this issue, see Benjamin (1989). See also Lenhart (1995) for an overview of recent research on sea nomads.
4   This is also partly due to the wide and discontinuous distribution of the Orang Laut. Unpublished works include, for example, Normala Manap (1983); Mariam Mohd. Ali (1984). Fragmented articles include: Sandbukt (1982); Wee (1985, 1988); Lenhart (1995, 1997); Chou (1995, 1997); Sather (1995, 1998, 1999).
5   See for example Logan (1847b); Thomson (1847a, 1847b); Hill (1973); Skeat and Ridley (1973); Gibson-Hill (1973).
6   Sopher (1977:174) also mentions how writers on the Orang Laut have expressed shock and disgust at the sea nomads' lack of sanitation. The sea nomads often accumulate 'slops and offal of all kinds' in 'the bilge a few inches away from the people on board.' However, Sopher explains that there is probably a practical reason for keeping refuse on board while at sea. This is to prevent sharks from being attracted to the boats.
7   This differs from the situation in Malaysia where indigenous communities are constitutionally defined as non-Malay aborigines. This is in contrast to the indications of Major William-Hunt (1952) -- the former Colonial Adviser on aborigines -- that there was no definite or rigid difference between 'Malays' and 'Aborigines' in British Malaya.

Nevertheless, in Malaysia, 'Malays' and 'Aborigines' are now legally differentiated into two distinct categories in the amended Federal Constitution of 1981, Article 160(2). 'Malayness' thus specifically excludes *orang asli* (aborigines). The view of my Indonesian informants reflects opinions of the earlier period in Malaya when 'Malays' and 'Aborigines' were not yet clearly differentiated into mutually exclusive categories.

8 There is some speculation in conjectural prehistory that boat-dwelling nomadism was a secondary development out of an original land-dwelling nomadism. (Dunn and Dunn, 1984:264-67; Wee, 1985:627-32)

9 See, for instance, Benjamin (1989); Mariam Mohd. Ali (1984); Normala Manap (1983); Pang (1984).

10 Wee (1985:54) refers to them as *bangsa lain* (other stock).

Chapter 2

The Setting

Picture 2: Journeying through the Archipelago with the Orang Laut

RIAU

'Riau' is officially recognized by the Indonesian government as one of Indonesia's twenty-seven provinces. It comprises Riau *daratan* (mainland) in the central part of the east coast of Sumatra, and Riau *kepulauan* (island) which stretches from the Strait of Malacca in the west to the South China Sea and Borneo in the east. Together, mainland and island Riau cover 94,562 square kilometres. Occupying Riau is a diverse population of 2,842,955 comprising Malays, Javanese, Bawenese, Minangkabau, Buton, Buginese, Flores, Chinese, and aboriginal groups such as the Orang Laut, Orang Dalam, and Orang Akit (Pemerintah Daerah Tingkat I Riau, 1994:5).

Within the bureaucratic structure of Indonesia, Riau is located at the lowest administrative level, far removed from the national centre Jakarta. In 1945, Sukarno declared Indonesia an independent Republic; however, this news did not reach Riau, and it was not until 1950 that Riau finally came under direct Indonesian administration.[1]

Historically and culturally, the Riau Archipelago has been and continues to be a part of the Malay World (*Alam Melayu*).[2] This is a territory based upon a network of genealogically related kingdoms. Geographically, the Malay World includes present-day peninsular Malaysia, Singapore, the east coast of Sumatra, the coast of Borneo from Brunei westwards to Banjarmasin, and the Riau Archipelago. These kingdoms, some extinct and others still existing, are currently divided among the five nation-states of Indonesia, Malaysia, Singapore, Brunei, and Thailand.[3] The Malay World thus extends beyond the borders of the Republic of Indonesia. It does, however, exclude parts of the Indonesian state such as Java, Bali, and the eastern islands (Wee, 1985:59-62).

The Riau Archipelago approximately correlates with the area that once constituted the territory of the Riau-Lingga Sultanate (1722-1911).[4] This Sultanate, a coalition of Malay and Buginese dynasties, was an ethnically segmented and socio-politically stratified society. The Riau Archipelago became a centre of power when the Riau-Lingga Sultanate established its court there.[5] In 1911 the Riau-Lingga Sultanate collapsed when the Dutch forced the then reigning Sultan Abdul al-Rahman into abdication.[6] Penyengat island was the last capital of the Riau-Lingga Sultanate.

Sitting at 'the bottleneck for the movement of culture and the passage of trade' (Sopher, 1977:365) between India, Southeast Asia, and China, the Riau Archipelago saw its heyday in regional and international commerce during the early Malay kingdoms (Andaya, 1997:484-8). This dynamism petered out with 'the founding of Singapore in 1819, the subsequent Anglo-Dutch Treaty of 1824, and the gradual imposition of colonial rule' (Andaya, 1997:494-5). The British in setting up neighbouring Singapore as a free trade post in 1819 siphoned off most of the trade that had formerly gone to Riau (Dobbin 1983:104, 176, 219). Problems compounded for Riau when it lost parts of its territory in the Anglo-Dutch Treaty of 1824, which divided the old kingdom of Johor into a British and Dutch zone. The British 'sphere of influence' comprised the Malay peninsula, Singapore, and the intervening islands, while the Dutch zone included the Riau-Lingga Archipelago, eastern Sumatra, and the Pulau Tujuh (Andaya, 1997:495). Riau spiralled further into obscurity as a peripheral region for decades in the independent Indonesian state (Mubyarto, 1997:542).

It was only in late December 1989 that Riau once again emerged into political and economic importance. The then Deputy Prime Minister of Singapore, Goh Chok Tong, proposed a trilateral economic programme among Singapore, Riau, and Johor of Malaysia. This programme, named the 'Growth Triangle,' aims at complementing and linking the three countries endowed with different comparative advantages to form a larger region with greater potential for growth (*Straits Times*, 21 December, 1989; Lee, 1991).[7] As a result of this programme, the Riau Archipelago is now divided into two administrative units, the subdistrict *Kabupaten Kepulauan* Riau and the municipality *Kotamadya* Batam. Both continue to be parts of the Province of Riau although *Kotamadya Batam* has been given autonomous administrative status as an area for industrial development.

The Riau Archipelago is a maze of over 3,200 islands. This is a difficult and confusing area for a novice. On maps, some islands are named and others are not. To complicate matters, locals have their own names for these islands. Sometimes the location of a place name may also differ between the cartographers and the locals. Thus, what may be the site for Dapur Enam on the map may well differ in location from the perspective of the locals. Until one is familiar with the area, one may easily find oneself confusing places and place names when discussing locations with a local. No commercial boats ply to most of these islands. In order to reach any place, it is necessary to find one's way into the local and private network of fishing boats that operate in the Archipelago. Hitching a ride on these private boats poses another challenge, as more often than not, these boats do not adhere to fixed schedules.

THE ORANG LAUT

The Orang Laut are found scattered throughout the Riau-Lingga Archipelago of Indonesia and the southern coasts of the Malay Peninsula (Johor), the east coast of Sumatra, and the larger islands of Bangka and Belitung

(Sandbukt, 1982:17).[8] Until recently, they were also to be found along the north coast of Singapore (Mariam, 1984).[9]

Historically, the Orang Laut played a pivotal role in establishing the position of the Sultan during the Malacca-Johor and Riau-Lingga Sultanate.[10] Within the former Malay feudal system, the Orang Laut were divided into various *suku* or clans, such as *Suku* Tambus, *Suku* Galang, *Suku* Mantang, and *Suku* Barok.[11] Different clans occupied different territories with each assigned a different task in serving the ruler and ranked accordingly (Andaya 1975a:7; Sopher, 1977:92-114). The clans collectively formed the *orang kerahan* (nobility's vassals). Their tasks or duties were wide ranging. Some fought crucial wars for the Sultan; others provided the nobles with marine products such as *tripang* (sea cucumbers), pearls, and seaweed as well as bird's nests. These products were important export items for international trade, and China was an important importer of these items (Vos, 1993:121-8).

Clans which attached themselves to the centres of power thrived and rose in political positions, but at the same time came under stricter control of the central power. In contrast, clans which were geographically far removed from the centre, and which were accordingly ranked lower in status, were actually best able to retain their autonomy. These were the clans that the Malay lords found most difficult to control, so they were often much freer from feudal obligations. Some of these clans were not even regarded as subjects. They were able to live relatively independent lives, subject only to the leadership of their respective tribal chiefs (*batin*).

In the eighteenth century, with the emergence of the Dutch and the weakening of the Sultanate, the political importance of the Orang Laut started to decline.[12] In the nineteenth century, members of the Malay ruling class who had lost their positions of power would turn to the lucrative business of piracy. This was possible only if they secured the support of some Orang Laut loyalists. The Suku Galang in particular served most prominently in this respect.[13]

The traditional polities into which the Orang Laut were feudally organized and socially ranked no longer exist today. Nevertheless, they still organize themselves into separate clans occupying different islands and moorage areas throughout the Archipelago. Nowadays, they no longer speak of themselves as *Suku* Tambus or *Suku* Galang, etcetera. Rather, they are more keen to identity themselves as belonging to certain territories. They now identity themselves as Orang Pulau Nanga (a person from Nanga island) or Orang Teluk Nipah (a person from Teluk Nipah). The distinction of belonging to different territories is strongly stressed by all groups. Pulau Nanga and Teluk Nipah are two islands in the Galang area, occupied by two different groups. These islands are in such close proximity that they are within hailing distance. Yet the members of both communities are adamant that they be recognized as different groups occupying distinct territories. Each territory also acknowledges a different *kepala* (head), and different groups respect each other's collective tenure of territorial ownership which is based on kinship lines (Chou, 1997).

Today, the *Kantor Sosial* (Social Office) in Tanjung Pinang, Riau, estimates the Orang Laut population as comprising 1,757 males and 1,652 females (1993, oral communication). This constitutes approximately 0.6% of the total 565,000 population in the Riau Archipelago, of which the Malays form the great majority. The given figures for the Orang Laut are, however, highly disputable. In the course of my fieldwork, I found it impossible to reconcile officially registered figures with the census that I had recorded. The mobile economies of the Orang Laut, the lack of official recording of births and deaths in the outer islands of the Archipelago, the inaccessibility to the public of existing government reports, and the attempts by government officials to lower the figures for what are deemed the backward sectors of Indonesian society which are a source of embarrassment to a modern and progressive state are among the numerous reasons for the hazy population figures for the Orang Laut.[14]

The sea and coastal fringes have been the life and living spaces for the Orang Laut for centuries. From birth, they have been exposed to living on the sea. Accordingly, they possess an outstanding knowledge of the winds, currents, and tides that govern the sea, of the location of rich fishing grounds and mangrove swamps, and of the position of the sun, moon, and stars by which to navigate their way through the Archipelago. The sea provides the Orang Laut with their main source of food. From time to time, they supplement their diet with other maritime products such as shell-fish and crabs collected along the strand, as well as with fruits and animals which they collect and hunt from forests. Surplus maritime produce is sold to the Chinese *thau-ke*s (middlemen).[15] The use of spears is a distinctive fishing method of the Orang Laut. They manifest great resourcefulness in constructing their own fishing gear, which apart from spears includes harpoons, fishing lines, and baskets (Chou, 1997:619-23). Apart from fishing, some Orang Laut also accept seasonal commissions from Chinese *thau-ke*s to chop wood from mangrove swamps for the production of charcoal.

Some groups of Orang Laut have either voluntarily settled or been pressured to settle on land, and now live in government houses or self-constructed dwellings along the coast (Lenhart, 1977:585-9). Nevertheless, they still return to live on board their *sampan*s (boats) with their entire families when they embark on fishing voyages. A fishing voyage may last from a night to a few months.

The senior male member of a clan is often chosen as the *Kepala* (Head) of the community.[16] The Head is acknowledged to hold greater but not absolute authority over the community. Government authorities usually officially recognize his leadership; he is the one called upon to represent his community on formal occasions such as visits from government or religious officials to the community. The Orang Laut informed me that their Head was officially placed under the authority of the Head of the Malays in the region. This clearly indicates the subordinate political status of the Orang Laut in relation to the Malays. Although the Head of a clan is often verbally acknowledged and officially recognized to be a male, it is not uncommon to find that the actual power to make and carry out decisions on a daily basis as well as on crucial matters lies with a woman. Rights to ownership and division of labour are not clearly defined by sex. On fishing expeditions, men often spear fish, while women row the boats. These tasks are deemed complementary, and it is also not uncommon to hear men praise their women for being skilful spearers of maritime products (Chou, 1995:175-98). Both men and women possess the potential to become *dukun*s (practitioners of indigenous medicine), and there is almost no distinct division as to the types of *ilmu* (magic) they can practise.

Notes

1 According to Ricklefs (1981:202): 'As news spread of the declaration of independence, many Indonesians far from Jakarta disbelieved it ... It was well into September 1945 before the fact that independence had been declared was known in remoter regions.'
2 The most important document for understanding the origins of Riau is the great Malay epic that has come to be called the *Sejarah Melayu*, and which is best known for its version dated 1612 (Windstedt, 1938; Brown, 1953). Historians generally acknowledge that the *Sejarah Melayu* is a work of literature rather than a historical document in the western tradition. Nonetheless, in presenting a Malay perception of their past it also provides insights for scholars seeking explanations of historical developments.
3 See Andaya and Andaya (1982:37-113) on the historical relationships between the Sultanates.
4 Prior to this, the Riau Archipelago was a marginal area of the Malacca-Johor Sultanate (1400-1699). This Sultanate was ruled by a Malay dynasty comprising descendants of the Palembang (Srivijaya) ruling house who resided in the Malayan peninsula (Wolters, 1970:77-107).

5 The Riau-Lingga Sultanate was reigned over by the Malay sultans of Abd al-Jalil descent (who had included the Prime Minister and later successor of the last Sultan of the Malacca-Johor dynasty), and their Buginese viceroys of Opu Tendriburang Daeng Riaga descent (who had been the heads of the Buginese and who had helped the Abd al-Jalil dynasty to attain and retain power (Wee, 1985:597). Although from 1784 to 1787 there were already some Dutch residencies in the territory of the Sultanate, the last sultan of Riau was forced to abdicate as late as 1911. However, from the sixteenth century until the middle of this century the European colonial powers continuously succeeded in dominating trade and politics in the region and in weakening the power of the local rulers, before they finally replaced the native dynasties. For more on the history of the Riau-Lingga Sultanates, see Andaya (1975a), Andaya and Andaya (1982), Brown (1953), Tarling (1963), Tate (1971), Trocki (1979), Wee (1985), Winstedt (1956, 1979), Wolters (1967, 1970). On ethnic segmentation and political and social stratification of the Riau-Lingga Sultanate, see Logan (1847a:336), Schot (1882:161-5, 472-3; 1884:555-8), Sopher (1977:90, 93, 269), Wee (1985:168-220, 235-302).
6 Riau-Lingga was one of the last areas to come directly under the government of the Dutch East Indies. However, prior to 1911, there was already a Dutch presence in the Riau Archipelago. Except for 62 years at the beginning of the Riau Sultanate (that is, 1722-84), and 23 years during the Napoleonic Wars (1795-1818), a Dutch Residency had co-existed with the Sultanate since 1784. By the early twentieth century, however, the Dutch government in Batavia felt that there was little need to continue to share their power with the traditional rulers of Riau-Lingga (Wee, 1985:137-8).
7 The 'Growth Triangle' is also commonly known by the acronym 'Sijori,' which refers to the three sides of the Triangle: *Si*ngapore, *Jo*hor in Malaysia, and the *Ri*au Islands in Indonesia. The origins of the Growth Triangle as a concept is explained by Macleod and McGee (1996:424):

In the mid-1980s Singapore increasingly began to turn to Indonesia and the Riau islands as alternatives to the city's long-time dependence on Johor as an 'offshore' source of low-cost land, labour, and most critically, water (Singapore is dependent on outside sources for virtually all of its water supply). The increasing rapprochement between Jakarta and Singapore and the beginnings of joint initiatives in the Riaus in turn caused concern and some resentment in Johor. It became apparent that relations between Johor and Singapore could become threatened by the new relationship with Batam (part of the Riau province). To mollify this emerging grievance and to expand and push for further cooperation,

Singapore's then first Deputy Prime Minister, Goh Chok Tong, put forward the idea of a 'Triangle of Growth.' This idea was arrived at integrating Batam, Singapore, and Johor in a collaborative push for joint development on a regional scale.

8 Sopher (1977:51) lists three subdivisons of sea nomads of Southeast Asia as the Orang Laut, the Moken or Selung and the Bajau. The locations of the Moken and the Bajau have been recorded as follows. The Moken are said to be scattered around the Mergui Archipelago in the Tenasserim province of Burma as well as the chain of islands along the southwest coast of Thailand. On the other hand, the Bajau are known to be dispersed around the Philippine Sulu Archipelago, the neighbouring north coast of Borneo, the coastal waters of Sulawesi and the surrounding islands, and parts of the Flores Archipelago (Sandbukt, 1982:17).

9 The Orang Laut of Singapore were considered as undesirable citizens by the Singapore government because of what was deemed as their backward and unprogressive lifestyle of living in house boats. Local government policies thus forced the Orang Laut to either leave Singapore or to give up their way of life for urban flat dwellings. Most of the Orang Laut who left Singapore are now to be found in the Riau-Lingga Archipelago of Indonesia.

10 In sources of the sixteenth to the nineteenth centuries, the ancestors of the present Orang Laut appear under the collective terms of Celates (a Portuguese term probably derived from the Malay *selat*, 'straits,' which might be translated as 'people of the straits'), Orang Laut (sea people), or Orang Pesukuan (people of the divisions). In practice, these terms were applied to a various groups of sea nomads and other coastal populations (Sopher 1977:53, 266, 326-7; Andaya 1975b:44). Only a few sources differentiate the indigenous population of the Archipelago, that is the Proto-Malayan sea nomads, from their sedentary descendants and the sedentary coastal Malays (Schot 1882, 1884).

11 For more on this issues, see Sopher, 1977 and Sandbukt, 1982.

12 See for example, Brown (1953), Tarling (1963), Wolters (1970) for a detailed discussion on how the Orang Laut declined in political importance.

13 On the role of the Orang Laut in the Malacca-Johor and the Riau-Lingga Sultanates, see Lummer (1993:5-26), Andaya (1975b), Brown (1953), Logan (1847a), Schot (1882), Sopher (1977), Tarling (1963), Tate (1971), Trocki (1979), and Wolters (1970). On piracy in the Malay World, see Andaya and Andaya (1982:131), Lummer (1992:139-42), Tarling (1963:1, 10-11, 39, 123), and Trocki (1979).

14 See Colchester (1986:89) and Chou (1997:608-10) for the official definition of Orang Laut communities.
15 See Embree (1973) for the spelling of Chinese terms.
16 It has been recorded elsewhere (see for example Sopher, 1977) that the leader of the Orang Laut is also addressed as *batin*.

CHAPTER 3
RANKING IN RIAU

Picture 3: The royal mosque on Penyengat Island

The Malays continue to perceive and map Riau as part of the wider Malay World. A system of social ranking prominent in the Malay society of Riau during the era of the Sultan continues to pervade intergroup relations with the Orang Laut today. Through the signs of purity that are perceived by the Malays, contrasting meanings of purity and impurity in one's Malayness are expressed in establishing group boundaries. These boundaries have become starker with the Orang Laut's redefinition and attribution of different meanings to the signs of purity observed by the Malays. Against this backdrop, inter- and intra-group relations underpinned by such hierarchical boundaries have found expression in different forms of exchange.

THE HIERARCHY OF RANKS

My Orang Laut and Malay informants speak of five different periods of political domination that the Riau Archipelago has come under.[1] They are the periods of the *Batin* (Chief), the Sultan,[2] the Dutch (1911-42), the Japanese (1942-5), and the Republic of Indonesia (1949 to the present), respectively.[3] Although the Riau Archipelago is currently a part of the Republic of Indonesia, it is the era of the Sultan which remains most significant to the Malay aristocrats. They continue to use the title Raja and to see Riau as part of the wider Malay World. Both the Orang Laut and the Malays are aware that reigning sultans still exist in other parts of the Malay World, such as in Brunei and Peninsular Malaysia.

Anderson's (1990:15) concept of nation states discusses the idea of imagined communities where 'the members ... will never know most of their fellow-members, meet them or even hear of them, yet in the minds of each lives the image of their communion.' Although Anderson was referring to the creation of nation states, parallels can be drawn with the situation in Riau. There is at present no sultanate in Riau, nor are there extensive contacts between my informants and other aristocrats in the wider Malay World. Nevertheless, my Riau aristocrat informants continue to conceive a unity with the royal houses of the wider Malay World which is, in turn, seen as belonging to the *umat* (nations of Islam).

In Pulau Penyengat, a genealogical chart demonstrating the position and links of the Riau aristocrats to the wider Malay World is prominently displayed in a public gallery. During the course of my fieldwork, my Malay aristocrat friends were often very eager to sketch from memory their genealogical charts to show me their lineage relationship to the royal houses. Genealogical charts and other royal heirlooms such as *keris*es (wavy double-bladed daggers), trays, and dinner sets bearing the royal insignia were often displayed or kept in their homes, ready to be shown to anyone. For the aristocrats, these are proofs of their royal descent and links to the wider Malay World. Several of my aristocrat informants have even used these charts in an attempt to gain admittance to the current royal palaces of Malaysia. Upon the establishment of a link, they enjoy the honour of receiving cards bearing royal greetings and invitations for special occasions. A Raja informant proudly showed me photographs of the informal meals to which he had been invited by members of the aristocracy in Peninsular Malaysia.

The keenness of the aristocrats to speak of and to show such things to others bespeaks their desire to present an identity of pure Malayness to others. They consider themselves to be the pure Malays because of their *keturunan* (descent) and *asal* (place of origin). It is their view that a person's Malayness stems from membership through patrilineal descent from specific Malay communities. This is also their basis for perpetuating a cleavage in ethnic identity between themselves and those whom they regard as impure Malays. The Malay aristocrats therefore view social relationships in Riau in terms of a system of ranking and the relative position in this system of their own *derajat* (rank).[4] It is important to note that this system of ranking applies only to the *orang Melayu* (Malays) of Riau; the Chinese, Javanese, and Boyanese in Riau are excluded. As Anderson (1990) asserts, limitations and boundaries exist to demarcate even the largest of all imagined communities from other communities. Conversely, it can also be said that it is the recognition of outsiders that makes the Malay World visible and felt.

To this very day, such a ranking system influences those at the centre of the power structure who regard those at the periphery as impure Malays. Such a situation also stretches beyond Riau. As observed by Armstrong (1984:28), such ranking 'prominent in traditional [Malay] society, particularly with respect to royalty and the Islamic religion' continues to make an impact on social interactions carried out in 'modern Malay life' in other parts of the Malay World such as Malaysia.

This is how Raja Rahim explained the place of the Orang Laut as serfs, during the era of the Sultan in Riau:

> There are several groups of Orang Laut, such as the *Suku Mantang, Suku Tambus, Suku Bintan, Suku Temiang, Suku Ladi* and *Suku Barok*.[5] I cannot remember all the groups. During the era of the Sultan, each group was assigned different work duties for the Sultan.[6] For example, the *Orang Mantang* (Mantang people) rowed boats and the *Suku Ladi* carried water and chopped firewood. The importance of each group could be seen from the sort of work they did. But they all obeyed the Sultan. The Orang Laut always lived in the sea. They were near but away from the Sultan's palace.

This ranking system, seen from the top down, is derived from the era of the Sultan (Armstrong, 1984; Gullick, 1988) and can be summarized in the illustration below.

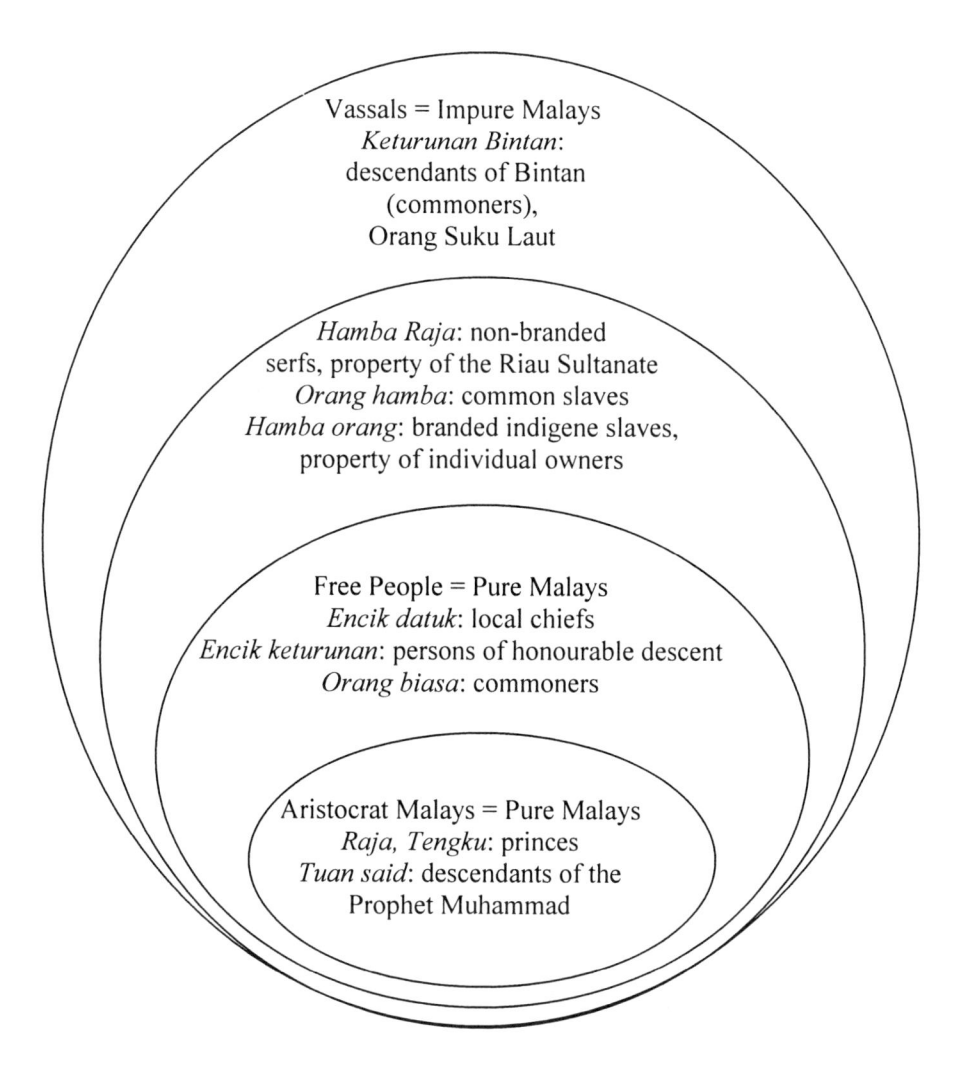

Vassals = Impure Malays
Keturunan Bintan: descendants of Bintan (commoners),
Orang Suku Laut

Hamba Raja: non-branded serfs, property of the Riau Sultanate
Orang hamba: common slaves
Hamba orang: branded indigene slaves, property of individual owners

Free People = Pure Malays
Encik datuk: local chiefs
Encik keturunan: persons of honourable descent
Orang biasa: commoners

Aristocrat Malays = Pure Malays
Raja, Tengku: princes
Tuan said: descendants of the Prophet Muhammad

Figure 1: Concentric representations of positions of rank influencing social interaction in the Malay World as perceived by the aristocrat Malays in Riau.

The Orang Laut were therefore the indigenous people in the political periphery. They could and would be summoned to the Sultan at the political centre whenever their services were required. On the notion of power in Southeast Asia, Errington (1989) maintains that throughout hierarchical Southeast Asia the ruler is regarded as the nucleus of the state. This supports Anderson's (1972) description of indigenous notions of power in Indonesia. Anderson describes how the Javanese see power as concrete, homogenous, immutable, and not to be challenged. Much of what Anderson and Errington have said also applies to Riau as perceived by the aristocrats who expect all other Malays in the periphery to be oriented to the centre and believe that an ordered polity should be void of challenges regardless of any and all inequalities.

The aristocrats see the necessity of institutionalizing their power structure. They have therefore constructed ideas with which to give shape and meaning to the Malay World. As manifest descriptions of themselves, the aristocrats stipulate a set of signs of purity, which connote refinement, superiority, and authority. Correspondingly, the Orang Laut on the outer periphery of the ranking system are seen as the personification of impurity which represents coarseness, inferiority, and submission. The deliberate choice of these signs by the pure Malays is to inculcate the continuity of a particular system with a suitable historical past (Hobsbawm and Ranger, 1992).

However, the realization of such a concept of power depends on the efforts of the political supporters of the aristocrats who ideally must not exert themselves to retain their power (Keeler, 1987). These supporters, such as the Bugis adventurers during the era of the Sultan who entered into alliances and negotiations on behalf of the aristocrats, are regarded in this system as the 'middle people.' They mediated between the aristocrats and the 'small people' such as the Orang Laut (Wee, 1985:171). Titles were bestowed upon these middle people and political offices were also established for them to legitimize their authority – all privileges denied to the small people absolutely. Although the aristocrats in Riau no longer confer titles today, they seem to receive the support of the Indonesian government and authorities. Officials who visit Pulau Penyengat are normally directed to the aristocrats who will serve as their hosts.

PURITY

'Purity' for the aristocrat Malays is manifested through *agama* (religion), *adat* (proper behaviour), *bahasa* (language), and what is physical appearance. This view is also shared by the commoner Malays. The following criticism voiced by two Malays reflects common opinions of the Orang Laut.

> Zainal:
> The Orang Laut are Malays, but my view is that the Orang Laut are the lowest. They are dark skinned. They do not know anything about toilets or hygiene. They have a different language to the extent that neither you nor I would understand. They have no religion. But be careful. Never let the Orang Laut hear you criticize them. They are very powerful in *ilmu hitam* and like bewitching people, especially those who criticize them, into marrying them. The Orang Laut cannot survive on land. They will die. Even though the government has given them houses, they insist on returning to the sea.

> Mansur:
> You will hear the Orang Laut claiming to be Christians, Protestants or Catholics, or that they have *masuk Islam* (entered Islam). This is so only in name. They do not pray and they still eat pork. If they say that they are Christians, they do not go to church. They have no religion. When it is the Chinese New Year, the Orang Laut follow. When it is the Muslims' *Hari Raya* (a festival), they follow too. However, they do not follow the customs.

The Orang Laut are acknowledged by many Malays as the indigenous Malays of Riau. However, their status as indigenes is not enough for them to be accepted as pure Malays. This is because they are deemed to have 'no religion,' speak a coarse language, lack a proper code of conduct, and lack refined physical appearance.

ISLAMIZATION

Islam in particular is used by the pure Malays as a vehicle for the legitimizing of authority, and hence also of superiority.[7] A person's purity depends on the observance of the following Islamic practices (Wee, 1985:573):

1. circumcision;
2. abstinence from pork and alcohol;
3. observance of Islamic burial principles;
4. pronouncement of the two statements of the testimonial creed;
5. marrying and divorcing in an Islamic manner;
6. ritual purification;
7. learning how to pray;
8. residing in a village with a mosque;
9. communal prayers on the two major Muslim festivals of *Hari Raya Puasa* and *Hari Raya Haji*;
10. communal prayers every Friday;
11. observance of the Islamic fasting month;
12. giving *zakat* and *fitrah*, the two types of Islamic alms;
13. praying privately five times a day; and
14. going on a pilgrimage to Mecca.

A person is formally converted to Islam upon pronouncing the testimonial creed in the presence of two Muslim witnesses. However, from the perspective of the local Islamic Malays, this is insufficient, hence the refusal to accept the Orang Laut as pure Muslims who have formally entered Islam. Two distinct contexts of centripetal orientation are implied here. One is the context of the world-wide Islamic *umat*, 'congregation of believers' or 'nation of Islam,' where all are supposed to be centripetally oriented towards God.[8] The other is the local *umat* in the shape of the bygone Sultanate, with Penyengat as its centre.

Pulau Penyengat was the capital of the Riau Sultanate.[9] Ever since the institution of the caliphate after the Prophet's death, it has been an established principle of Islamic organization that the ruler is also the religious leader of his polity. The ruler's authority was thus deemed to be divinely sanctioned. Therefore, the Sultan of Riau was regarded as the *Amir al-mu'munin* (Commander of the faithful) and *iman* (religious guide) (Farah, 1970:154). The political capital was also the religious centre (Matheson, 1989; Wee 1985:530). Early in the nineteenth century, Penyengat was described as *Serambi Mecca* (Gateway to Mecca). In the latter half of the century, it was also called *Pulau Indera Sakti*. When translated, *Indera* means royal while *Sakti* means sacred or divine supernatural power (Matheson, 1989:163-4). Towards the end of my field stay in 1992, I was approached by a Raja in Penyengat who was anxious that I purchase a recent publication of the history of Penyengat entitled *Pulau Penyengat Indera Sakti.*

My pure Malay informants clearly believe in the relevance of calling this former royal centre 'Pulau Penyengat Indera Sakti.' This belief rests upon various historical remains and is manifested in several ways. The enduring focus of Penyengat has undoubtedly been the mosque. My informants point out that this mosque is painted a distinct royal yellow as a constant reminder of its difference and importance. This mosque continues to be one of the main centres for Muslim marriages in Riau. It can be said that the Penyengat mosque is the most important of all mosques. Penyengat also has the highest incidence of things that are *keramat* (endowed with supernatural power) (Wee, 1985:323-405).[10] According to my informants, some royal graves are *keramat*.[11] As discussed by Endicott (1991:93), it is believed that the persons in *keramat* graves are 'not really dead.' These graves are called *makam* (grave), rather than *kubur* (grave), to distinguish them from ordinary graves. When I confused the terms during the initial stages of my fieldwork, even my Orang Suku Laut informants reminded me that most *makam*s are in Penyengat.

Before commencing my journey through Riau, I was told by the Malays to visit the *makam* of Raja Hamidah.[12] The intention, as they explained, was to seek permission to enter and stay in Riau. My advisers related numerous stories of how those who had failed to do so always encountered untoward circumstances of some sort. Midway through a visit from friends who had come to join me in the field, the Malays grew frantic with worry for the well-being of my visitors. They had forgotten to remind me that all guests on short stays – even if they were English and Scottish – had first to seek the permission of Raja Hamidah before venturing any further. Fortunately, to the relief of everyone, I had faithfully taken my guests to the *makam*. I was also often reminded to return to Penyengat upon the success of my studies to wrap the gravestones of their ancestors with cloth. I was told that even if I could not personally make it to Penyengat, I should arrange for the gravestones to be covered. The act of wrapping the gravestones with cloth can be understood as an exchange of a wish fulfilled with a wish offered – that is, my wish for protection is fulfilled by the blessing of the deceased and, in return, I offer the deceased a wish for his benefit (Wee, 1985:336).

Malays throughout Riau make pilgrimages to these *makam*s if they have special requests. Below is a Raja's wife's explanation of how Rokiah, a woman from Tanjung Pinang, had her request for a baby granted after her visit to Raja Hamidah's *makam*.

Rokiah came to see me one day. She had been married for two years and had been trying very hard to have a baby. She was very sad and worried that she could not conceive. I told her to go to Raja Hamidah's *makam*. She obeyed and not long after, she gave birth to a beautiful baby. It was like that. People have had all sorts of needs fulfilled.

This account shows that certain things associated with royalty – such as the mosque and *makam*s in Penyengat – are endowed with supernatural power. This power is viewed as untainted and pure because it is legitimized by Islam. These things in Penyengat continue to be visual representations of a kingdom today. The relationship between the power-endowed things and the pure Malays can be seen in various ways. Firstly, the concentration of so many Islamic things legitimizes Penyengat's central position in the Malay World. Secondly, they establish the island as the Gateway to Mecca. Thirdly, they authenticate the place as *Pulau Penyengat Indera Sakti*. Fourthly, they are in close proximity of, and easy access to, the aristocrats who make their residence in Penyengat. The aristocrats are able to pray regularly and participate in events at the mosque, and to visit the *makam*s regularly to perform Islamic rituals.

Parallels can be drawn with Anderson's (1972) study of the Javanese tradition. He mentioned the ruler's need to concentrate around himself things and people endowed with unusual power so that the power of these things would be absorbed and added to himself. The loss of these things and people would be interpreted as a diminution of the king's power and perhaps signal an impending collapse of the dynasty. Unlike the Javanese case, the constant contact with these things in Penyengat does not mean a direct absorption or addition of power for the pure Malays. Rather, the acts of Islamic piety add to their sense of purity which leads to superiority and power. Regular visits to the *makam*s mean that the pure Malays are more blessed, and the aristocrats acknowledge and reconfirm their descent. The continued links with their ancestors means the inheritance of power.

Proper Behaviour

The Malays also regard *adat*, which can be translated as proper behaviour or customs, as a reflection of a person's purity. However, proper behaviour is predicated upon Islamic principles. The following censure of the Orang Laut by a Malay clearly illustrates this concern.

Pindah:
Den will tell you that he has two wives. In actual fact, he has three or four others. He is too embarrassed to talk about those wives because he did not marry them in accordance with proper Malay behaviour. I can still remember how Den married his first wife. His wife wore a *sarong* (sheath dress) tied around her chest and then he chased her around the boat thrice. After that, they both swam in the sea.

All of them were drunk because they had been drinking liquor. There was no *kenduri* (religious feast). After that, the two of them entered a house and slept together. When they left the house, they got into a boat together and rowed away to go fishing. That was how they were considered a married couple. It is only now that they follow proper Malay behaviour when they marry. They go to the *iman* to obtain a marriage certificate. In the past, they would only follow the person. For the Suku Oyol, both male and female would dive beneath the boat and try to catch each other.[13] If they meet underwater, it means they are suited for marriage, if not it means they are not suited for one another.

I have never personally witnessed any Orang Laut marriage take place in the ways described above. Neither did my Orang Laut informants ever narrate their marriages in such terms. What is important here is that the Malays do not perceive the Orang Laut as marrying in proper Malay fashion. Nonetheless, I had on numerous occasions either been told by the Orang Laut themselves or witnessed how Orang Laut would *lari* (elope) and return to their respective families and be considered married. Saya, an Orang Laut from Pulau Abang, told me that she had initially disapproved of her daughter Joya's desire to marry Pri. Saya missed her daughter but was sure that Joya had eloped with Pri to Pulau Nanga. Together with the other members of her family, she went to see Joya. Saya explained that since Joya was already living with Pri, the matter was considered settled. There was no need for a ceremony of any sort. Everyone, including Saya and her family, accepted Joya as Pri's wife.

In another case, Lampung from Pulau Nanga left for Tiang Wang Kang within weeks of his wife Siti's death. He had told his siblings that he was seeking the help of a *dukun* (shaman) in Tiang Wang Kang to trace the identity of the person who had poisoned Siti. A week after Lampung's departure, I left on another boat with the other members of his family for Tiang Wang Kang. Upon our arrival, we were told that Lampung had arrived with the intention of marrying Simmon. She was from a nearby island. Lampung had not informed his family of his desire. This was because it was not permissible to marry within a hundred days after the death of one's spouse. His family refused him any assistance. They were certain that their eldest brother Bolong, who was also Head of the Orang Laut of Pulau Nanga, would be angered. I returned to Pulau Nanga with the other Orang Laut before Lampung did. In the meantime, Lampung and Simmon had started to sleep together and to form a working partnership in the same boat. When they at last arrived in Pulau Nanga, they were considered married. From the point of view of the Orang Laut, it is considered proper for a man and woman who have slept together and formed a permanent working partnership to be regarded as married. However, the Malays do not consider any such behaviour proper if it is not based upon Islamic principles. As failure to have an *iman* solemnize one's marriage is unacceptable, the Orang Laut are constantly mocked for creating their own standards of behaviour.

> Pindah:
> Suri puts a pail of water outside her house. She wants everyone to wash their feet in it before entering. She thinks that this will keep her house clean. What sort of custom is this? This is not a Malay custom! It is just her way of doing things. (Laughs.) Your feet will be dirtier if you dip them into the water.

In cases like the above, individuals are looked down upon as creating their 'own ways' dictated by their own desires. Even if it is behaviour commonly shared by most, if not all, Orang Laut, it is still not regarded as custom or proper behaviour. Instead, the Orang Laut are simply viewed as impure, hence unrefined people who do not possess proper Malay behaviour. In contrast, the Orang Laut never hesitate to tell me about their customs and acknowledge that some customs of theirs, such as eating pork, are indeed different from the Malays. Many Orang Laut were ready to say that they had followed proper Malay behaviour, but like the Malays, they would direct me to the Penyengat aristocrats when I pressed them for information on the origins or details of what constituted proper behaviour. This shows that while the Malays and Orang Laut may differ in opinion as to whether or not the latter possess proper behaviour, they agree that it is the aristocrats who are the authorities on proper Malay behaviour.

LANGUAGE

The Malays mock the Orang Laut for being incomprehensible because they have a *bahasa lain* (different language) and thus 'speak differently.'[14] The Malays do not regard any of the *Bahasa Orang Suku Laut* (Orang Suku Laut languages) as related to *Bahasa Melayu* (the Malay language) at all. Suffice it to say that the pure Malays regard themselves as arbiters of the Malay language,[15] and that the Orang Laut who can speak *Bahasa Melayu* are seen as having taken steps towards being purer Malays.

INDIGENOUS STATUS

There exist internal differences within the group that identifies itself broadly as Malays. The aristocrat Malays claim purity, hence sovereignty over the Malay World. In a counter-claim, the Orang Laut argue for indigenous status, thus ownership and rights to the area where they live. The Orang Laut refer to themselves as *asli Melayu*, and view the aristocrats as *Melayu dagang* (foreign Malays). By the same logic used by the aristocrats, they argue that it is one's patrilineal descent that determines whether one is a foreign or indigenous Malay in Riau. Further rifts prevail in the relationships among the non-aristocrat Malays themselves.

The Orang Laut support their claim of aboriginality through orally transmitted history from their ancestors. Below is a collection of narratives told by the Orang Laut.

> Pak Meen from Teluk Nipah island:
> The history begins here. The Orang Laut have five languages, or you could say, five *bangsa* (nations/people). Many years ago in the kingdom, there was a sultan in Johor who together with his followers set sail in his *perahu* (a type of boat) for Temasik. Temasik is now called Singapore. The Sultan of Johor asked the Sultan of Bintan for help. The Sultan of Bintan said, 'It is better for us to ask the Sultan of Lingga for help.' When they reached Lingga, they enlisted the Sultan's help. In between, one of the Sultans said that they should ask the Orang Laut for help if they wanted to be certain of winning.
>
> From the very beginning, we Orang Laut were led by Panglima Ladi.[16] We had moved in the direction of being divided into different Orang Laut. But the name Panglima Ladi commanded the respect of every *bangsa* of the Orang Laut. There were and still are five *bangsa* of Orang Laut. These are the *Mantang Ace, Mantang Baro, Mantang Mapor, Mantang Tambus,* and *Mantang Seme*.[17] To continue with the history, everyone agreed to go to Johor to help the Sultan of Johor. We went to help him get back what was seized from him. After that, the Sultan of Bintan, the Sultan of Daik, and all the Orang Laut returned to their own places. It was not long before the Sultan of Johor returned again because his purpose was to go to war. His

intentions indicated that he wanted us to work alongside him or be considered foreigners. Panglima Ladi knew only too well what all this meant. So, the Orang Laut hated the Sultan of Johor. This was because if the Orang Laut helped, they would be made to do all the work, while the Sultan of Johor would just enjoy all the success. From then on, we hated the Malays. They were bad influence. They could go alone.

From the very beginning, the Orang Laut had houses and we lived in the same village with the Malays. However, because of this matter, they hated us and we hated them; so we went down to our boats and fixed *kajang*s (movable sunshades of palm thatch).

Ceco from Pulau Nanga:
We came from Malaysia. Our ancestors were already Muslims, just like the Malays. When they moved here, they came in boats, so they were called Orang Laut. When they were in the boat, they forgot Islam. However, when they came to Indonesia, they started a village, and we returned to Islam. Hence, you can also say that the Orang Laut originated from Penyengat.

Sman from Dapur Enam island:
Raja Hamidah's descent was also from the Orang Laut. Formerly, we all lived in boats out at sea. We had no houses. If it had not been for us the indigenes, how could there be islands now? We say that we own all the islands. In our history, the *Raja Laut* (King of the Sea) had fifteen children.[18] He gave each of them rings and islands. That is how the islands came into being.

The above accounts vary greatly in detail. However, there are similar issues of concern underlying all of them. Firstly, there is the stress on origin from a single group who have shared the same habitat. Because of this, the Orang Laut believe it is only logical that they share a common descent with the Malays. Secondly, Islam was not the cause of the division. In fact, before the division, there are accounts which maintain that the Orang Laut were already Muslims. This directly questions the status of the pure Malays as the progenitors of Islam in the Malay World and consequently challenges the moral superiority of the Malays as leaders and guardians of Islam. However, it does show that the Orang Laut understand that the sedentary lifestyle, rather than a nomadic one, is more suitable for providing a home for Islam.[19] Thirdly, the islands including Penyengat in the Malay World were in fact opened up by the sea-faring activities of the Orang Laut who thus claim ownership of the area that they have settled. This undoubtedly challenges the Malays' notion of Penyengat's centrality in the Malay World. The Orang Laut dismiss Penyengat as a privileged centre of authority, nor do they believe that Raja Hamidah played a pivotal role in the establishment of Riau.

The stories told by the Orang Laut of their history must be contrasted with those told orally by the Malays. Below is a cross-section of narratives by the Malays on the beginnings of the Orang Laut.

Yusof:
The Orang Laut started out as one group. They are the indigenes of Riau. In one of the families, everyone died leaving only a surviving brother and sister. The brother married his sister. This couple were so ashamed that they went to stay in the boat out at sea. As a consequence, they did not have any religion. That was how two groups of people came into being ... one group in the sea and one group on land.

Fatimah:
The Orang Laut were actually also Malays and Muslims. That is why they look like us Malays. However, they committed some wrongdoing. Once the Prophet Muhammad asked this group of Malays to get him *ikan idip* (a fish). However, this group of Malays ate half of the fish before giving the other half to the Prophet. This angered the Prophet Muhammad so that he cursed them. That is how they ended up living in boats. As a result, they also threw away the Prophet Muhammad and now they don't have a Prophet.

Raja Rahim:
The Orang Laut are descended from three places, Daik-Lingga, Penyengat, and Johor. The Orang Laut are the aborigines. They are also Malays. Formerly, they were also Muslims. However, with their constant shifting from one place to another, there was not anyone to teach them Islam. As a result, they forgot Islam.

Long ago, there was a family who lived in a house on land. One day strong winds collapsed the house. Many in the family died. Those who managed to survive cursed those who had survived on land, so they left to live in the sea instead. They thought they would be able to move their boats into smaller rivers to seek refuge during seasons of strong winds.

The Orang Laut have advanced considerably now. They want to live in houses on land, and some may even possess their own motorized boats. The government has also helped to build houses for them.

While there are details that differ in the accounts above, there are also clear and important points of agreement. Firstly, the indigenous status of the Orang Laut in the Malay World is undisputed. This corresponds to the claims made by the Orang Laut. Secondly, although nobody denied the fact that the Malays and Orang Laut shared a common descent and religion, it was made clear that the division arose due to the Orang Laut's breach of Islamic principles and proper behaviour. The division thus arose between the coarse, sinful, and impure Malays and the refined, pious, and pure Malays. Thirdly, this division was based upon a difference in lifestyle: nomadic versus sedentary. Recalling the narratives of the Orang Laut, it seems that both hold the view that nomadism, as opposed to sedentism, is not conducive to upholding Islam.[20]

The indigenous status of the Orang Laut is undisputed. What remains in dispute is, however, the issue of power and a person's position in the hierarchy of being Malay in Riau.

WEAPONS OF THE WEAK

Scott (1985), in his study of the everyday forms of peasant resistance for the purpose of defending their interests, directed his attention to the Malaysian village of Sedeka. He focused on the economic and employment relations involved in class and ideological struggles between rich Malay landlords and poor landless Malays. Such struggles are not found in Riau; instead, the concerns of the Malays in Riau centre on two things: the setting up of ethnic boundaries and the imposition of changes into Orang Laut culture. Nevertheless, the Orang Laut's methods of resistance against domination are comparable to those of the Malaysian peasants.

I have shown how the idea of centralized power and purity work from top to bottom and that the Orang Laut resist such a view by claiming indigenous ownership of the Malay World. However, their resistance efforts are not an outright or collective challenge to the Malays, as such measures might actually work against them. They resist through ways which Scott (1985:29-34) has described as 'dissimulation, calculated conformity, false compliance, feigned ignorance and slander.' These forms of self-help resistance which require minimum or no planning often reap huge and immediate gains.

Today, the Orang Laut face immense pressures from the Malays to become Muslims. Efforts to convert them launched by the Indonesian government,[21] which often sends Islamic representatives to the communities to evangelize, further trouble the situation. The response, however, cannot be described as enthusiastic; as one Orang Laut in Pulau Abang says, 'We have yet to enter Islam. We are still waiting for someone to come.'

CALCULATED CONVERSION

The following is a case study of ongoing Islamic missionary activities carried out among the Orang Laut of Pulau Nanga, which reflects the calculated conformity of the Orang Laut to Islam. According to my Orang Laut informants, they entered Islam a few years prior to my arrival. They recounted how the Head of the Malay community from neighbouring Pulau Sembur, together with a government official named Pak Muji from Tanjung Pinang, had one day arrived to ask if they had any religion. They replied that they 'did not have any religion.' They were thereupon asked to become Muslims, with the assurance that they would be taken care of. They recalled how Pak Muji gave them planks of wood and nails to construct their houses on land. He visited and taught each family how to keep their house clean like the Malays. He also gave rice, sugar, soap, and cloths for purposes of prayer to every family in the community. The Orang Laut were promised that help would be rendered to bury their deceased in a proper manner and that they would be taught how to pray. A mosque and a school were also to be built in the community. The Orang Laut who agreed to enter Islam received much aid from Pak Muji in the early stages of their conversion, in contrast to the Christianized Orang Laut of the neighbouring island Teluk Nipah, who hardly received any help at all. The Orang Laut in both communities were told that they would receive wood and nails to construct houses on land even if they chose not to enter Islam. However, those in Teluk Nipah maintained that the wood and nails that they had received were hardly enough to meet their needs. To this Pak Muji had replied that there were simply not enough wood and nails left after meeting the needs of the Pulau Nanga community. The Pulau Nanga community also complained bitterly that, after the first stages of help given by Pak Muji, he had since become 'useless.' In spite of all the dissatisfactions, the Orang Laut were aware that as long as they remained officially recognized as having entered Islam, they could hope for visits and help, rare though they might be, from other or higher official Islamic institutions.

In the course of my fieldwork in Pulau Nanga, representatives of the Islamic School and Departments of Religions and Social Affairs arrived for a half-day visit. The Orang Laut once again were disgruntled when Pak Muji ordered them to give the village and their houses a general clean-up. They were also organized into building a jetty and contributing Rp. 500 per family to purchase bottled drinks for the guests. The Orang Laut complied with Pak Muji's instructions as they were anticipating distributions of clothes and food from their visitors. When the representatives arrived, bags of clothes were presented to Bolong and Ceco, the two eldest brothers who were Heads of the Orang Laut community. Unknown to others, Bolong instructed his siblings to remain silent and not ask questions of their guests. The more vocal siblings subsequently decided to bathe or go fishing during the visit, explaining that they had agreed to obey Bolong and reasoned that 'it was better' for them to observe from a distance lest they open their mouths. The visitors were completely unaware of the arrangement that had taken place behind their backs. They were thus under the impression that they had procured total allegiance from the Orang Laut in Pulau Nanga. At one point Bolong and Ceco, as representatives of the community, donned their *songkok* (rimless fez-like cap)[22] and followed their visitors in raising their hands during the prayer session. There were quiet whispers and muffled laughter among the congregation. It was clear to everyone that their representatives were experiencing great discomfort as they were 'not used to praying.' They told me that Ceco was better than Bolong at putting up a public front.

In the Islamic representatives' address, mention was made of the fact that the Orang Laut did not speak *Bahasa Melayu*. The representatives also pointed out that the Orang Laut did not have names that could be found in 'books.' Still, it was noted that upon conversion to Islam, they had now gained Islamic names such as 'Muhammad' and 'Ali.'[23] In the speech, promises were also made that a school and a mosque would be built on Pulau Nanga. The entire missionary zeal was therefore to Islamize the Orang Laut and to educate them in refined language and proper behaviour.

I had the opportunity of asking the visitors if they would be crossing over to help the Orang Laut on the neighbouring islands of Teluk Nipah or Abang, and received the following reply:

Official:
No. We were not given any instructions to go over there. Perhaps this is because the Orang Laut on Teluk Nipah are not Muslims. We did not even know there were Orang Laut on Pulau Abang. Are they Muslims?

Once again, the Orang Laut on Teluk Nipah had cause to be unhappy. Unlike their Pulau Nanga neighbours, they did not receive any help at all from these visitors.

Anticipating help upon entering Islam, many Orang Laut confided in me that 'there is nothing to lose' with the possible exception of abstinence from pork. In the months that I lived with my Islamized Orang Laut informants on Pulau Nanga, I was either taught or became quite aware through observation of their calculated forms of conformity.

LOCATION OF DWELLINGS

Midway through the first stretch of my fieldwork in 1992, Ross, an Orang Laut woman of Pulau Nanga, fell gravely ill. One of the reasons given for her illness was that her house was built on land, rather than over the sea. Although there were a few Malays who had built their houses over the sea, their reasons for siting their houses there differed from those of the Orang Laut. One of the reasons given by my Malay informants was that the coast was too congested and that they were forced to move out over the sea. Sopher (1977:1) has described a line that demarcates the strand and the sea as 'zone of transition.' He mentions how this zone of transition is 'very often characterized by its own special land forms and life forms.' Similarly, this line is perceived as a zone of cultural and ethnic transition for the Malays in Riau. The Malays were insistent that if the intention was to draw the Orang Laut into a progressive lifestyle, the latter should be made to construct their houses on land rather than over the sea. Also, the Malays believed that their success in getting the Orang Laut to build their houses on land could be correlated with a greater chance of Islamizing them. Not surprisingly then, the Malays felt that they were losing control and authority over those who persisted in choosing a nomadic sea-based lifestyle. On the other hand, the Orang Laut saw the matter very differently. They regarded houses on land as 'dirty.' They explained that this was because their graves are also on land. They believed that water from the graves would seep into the ground under their houses when it rained. Furthermore, people defecate and urinate on the open land.[24] When Ross recovered, her family tore apart their house and rebuilt it over the sea. This triggered off a slow but steady exodus of all land-based houses to the sea. The move was initially unnoticeable until most of the houses were rebuilt over the sea. It was only then that the Malays on surrounding islands began to comment that this clearly indicated that the Orang Laut could not survive on land and were reverting to their former lifestyle.

My Orang Laut informants explained that it had always been their intention to build their houses over the sea. When Pak Muji first gave them the construction materials, he had issued strict instructions that all houses had to be built on land. Pak Muji had warned that if they wanted to challenge this official policy, they would have to write to the government offices in Jakarta and Pekanbaru for permission. The Orang Laut felt intimidated at the thought of dealing with the authorities because of their illiteracy. Bolong, as Head of the Orang Laut, therefore agreed to Pak Muji's instructions and the others had no choice but to comply. The Orang Laut claimed that in relocating their houses back to the sea, they had in fact obeyed all initial instructions. They believed that it was time to move as it was beyond their control that people were falling ill. They reasoned that unless Pak Muji wanted to be answerable for all the deaths or provide effective medical aid, he could not fault them for moving their houses back to the sea. More importantly, they pointed out that they were unable to consult Pak Muji on this matter due to his infrequent visits to the community.

NON-PARTICIPATION

Another form of passive non-compliance by the Orang Laut on Pulau Nanga was evident during the *Hari Raya Puasa* (a religious festival after the fasting period) celebrations on the neighbouring Malay island of Sembur. As a rule, the Malays in Sembur avoid interacting with the Orang Laut; however, as they were obliged to host a *kenduri* during *Hari Raya Puasa* for all Muslims in the surrounding area, they had to include the Orang Laut.[25] To their disappointment, anger, and embarrassment, no Orang Laut appeared. When I asked the Orang Laut if they had reasons for not attending the *kenduri*, they shrugged and said they did not have enough eggs to make cakes for the *kenduri*. The Malays felt insulted by what they considered a poor excuse. The Malays maintained that they were not even expecting any contributions. As this was a period in which to celebrate the forgiveness of all wrongdoings, the Malays could not exhibit their anger even though they were certain that the Orang Laut simply did not attribute any importance to the event, and only cared about carrying on with their fishing activities.

EATING PORK

A prime concern in the conversion to Islam is the need to abstain from eating pork and drinking liquor. The Orang Laut are aware that they are constantly being watched and criticized as 'pork-eaters' by the Malays who, upon being pressed, would admit they cannot identify anyone in particular as they have never caught an Orang Laut in the act of buying or eating pork. In fact, pork is not a common food among the Orang Laut. There are several reasons for this. Firstly, there are those who sincerely obey the laws of Islam. Secondly, there are those who do not like the taste of pork. Thirdly, the meat is not easily available. Yet, for those who still desire pork despite having formally entered Islam, ways are devised for obtaining it with the assurance of remaining anonymous. The Orang Laut are often able to get pork by collaborating with their Chinese *thau-ke*s (bosses). My Orang Laut informants would often choose a time when there would be no Malays around to approach their *thau-ke*s whose families, as the Malays knew well, were pork-eaters. It is not at all unusual for an Orang Laut or anybody else to bring fish at all hours of the night to the *thau-ke*, and, having sold his or her fish, to make purchases for provisions from the *thau-ke*'s shop. The Orang Laut would thus seize this time as an opportunity to collect pork, as the shop was less crowded and it was very difficult to see the transaction in the dark. Often when the Chinese *thau-ke*s discovered that their Orang Laut *anak-buah* (followers/underlings) wanted the left-over pork from their religious feasts, they would arrange a late collection time. Tins of pork are also available from the Chinese *thau-ke*s. Ways are devised to enable the Orang Laut to walk away with the tins of pork safely. In one shop, the *thau-ke* kept all his tinned pork hidden beneath a counter. Whenever an Orang Laut asked for them, the *thau-ke* would, as an added precaution, remove all labels and wrap the tins in some other way. The Orang Laut also adopt the method of feigned ignorance in obtaining pork. The Chinese *thau-ke*s sell a variety of Chinese cakes during major Chinese festivals to the Chinese clients in the islands. The Malays believe that most of these cakes are made of lard, and have refused to buy them. However, the Orang Laut delight in these cakes. One day, while one of my Orang Laut informants was making a purchase, the *thau-ke* thought it his duty to inform her that the Malays considered this particular cake to contain lard. She smiled at him and replied, 'But they are not certain that it does, yeah? No one knows for sure.' The *thau-ke* gave an understanding smile and wrapped the cake in newspaper for her. She was thereafter a regular customer. In the same way, liquor is obtained from the Chinese. The Orang Laut would often tell me that 'a little liquor is good for the health.' There are also times when eating pork is difficult for the Orang Laut who have Malay spouses. In one such case, an Orang Laut woman who claimed to be Christian told me that she was going to invite her brother who had entered Islam over to eat pork.[26] I asked how this would be possible for he had already entered Islam. She said that her brother's wife, who was Malay, would not like it if he ate pork at home. However, she knew that he missed eating pork. She would therefore help him out periodically by inviting him over for a meal. Although he would be given advance information on what he was going to eat, she explained that, once seated, it would be considered very rude of him to refuse her food. She added that he always enjoyed his meal.

TRADING STORIES

The 'trading of stories' is another tool of resistance prevalent among the Orang Laut. Below are examples of stories told by my Orang Laut informants in a comparison of their position with that of the Orang Laut in Malaysia.

> Ceco:
> Look at the Orang Laut in Malaysia. We are the same. As the indigenous peoples of Malaysia, they are well provided for. The Orang Laut have been given motorized boats, nice houses, rice, money, motorcycles, and television sets. We know because people who have been to Malaysia have told us. There was once a television programme featuring the Orang Laut in Malaysia. We saw the place they lived in and their fishing equipment. They were given everything. They even had television aerials sticking out of their houses.

Ceco's younger brother, Boat, then retold this same story.

> Boat:
> Those who have been to Malaysia tell us of how the Orang Laut there receive assistance to get anything they want. They have been given not one, but two houses, two motorized boats ... they have enough. It is not like us here. We are not given anything!

If the Malays have looked to the wider Malay World, such as Malaysia, with stories to legitimize their kingship, the Orang Laut too have employed similar methods in justifying their indigenous status. They exchange stories of the privileged status of the Orang Laut there whom they 'have seen on television' or 'have heard from those who have been to Malaysia.' They claim that this is because the Malays there respect the indigenous status of the Orang Laut. These stories are intended to shame the Malays in Riau for their lack of respect and concern for their indigenous Malays.

The Orang Laut also express collective grievance against the Malays by telling stories of *jahat* (evil/wicked) Malays. To illustrate how evil the Malays are, the Orang Suku Laut often relate how the Malays even poison one another. The Orang Laut of Pulau Nanga had a favourite story to tell me. Some years prior to my fieldwork, the Malays of Pulau Sembur invited another group of Malays for a football match on Pulau Sembur. No Orang Laut was invited to play in the match. Soon after the match, there was an epidemic which killed most of the Malays of Sembur. The few surviving Malays fled Pulau Sembur in fear. Some even sought refuge by putting up movable sunshades of palm thatch over their boats and went out to live in the sea like the Orang Laut. Pulau Sembur became deserted except for the three Chinese families who remained in their homes. No Chinese died. According to my Orang Laut informants, this was because the Chinese, like the Orang Laut, had not participated in the football match. Their lives had thus been spared. Also, the Chinese are seen as having powerful deities that protect them even if the Malays want to harm them. The Orang Laut explained that the Malays of Sembur 'cheated' during the match. This antagonized their opponents, who decided to place a curse upon them.

The Orang Laut also laugh at how easy it is to fool the Malays. The Orang Laut are aware that the Malays use the criteria of physical appearance and speech to show their superiority. These criteria are easily manipulated to fool the Malays. The Orang Laut would often dress up and apply make-up when they travelled to Tanjung Pinang. Upon their return, they would have merry accounts of how the Malays had mistaken them for fellow Malays.

Beneath the safe disguise of outward compliance, the Orang Laut have developed many ways of resistance against the pressures exerted by the Malays on them to alter their lifestyle. They have effectively refused to conform to the standards of purity imposed upon them. Calculated conformity, false compliance, feigned ignorance, gossip, rumours, and jokes are all expressions of the actual degree to which the Orang Laut have accepted the code of conduct imposed upon them by the Malays. These are clear but safe indications of the Orang Laut's contempt for and defiance of the social order constructed by the Malays. In their own way, they are defining their conception of an alternative Malay World.

REDEFINING PURITY

Like many underprivileged groups elsewhere (e.g., Scott, 1985), the Orang Laut are aware of gaining short-term material benefits through their calculated conformity to the dominant ideology of the Malays. Some of them nevertheless refuse to be incorporated into the ideal Malay World of the pure Malays, but others – in particular, those who have been pressured into religious conversion – adopt a more moderate and selective manner of resistance. They have incorporated aspects of the ideology upheld by the Malays into their own system of social organization. This is comparable to the situation of gypsies in Southern England. As a subordinate group, the gypsies have incorporated 'symbols, rites and myths' from the larger society (Okely, 1983:77). So have the Orang Laut chosen to select and reject certain aspects of the dominant society's ideology. That which is adopted, then, takes on a new coherence which serves to accommodate the Orang Laut on two counts: to identify themselves as a group independent of the Malays and to rank, internally, the different groups of Orang Laut according to relative degrees of evilness. The criterion of religion is adopted as an indicator of their entry into the wider world. This also attests to their non-evilness, hence purity. The Malays focus specifically on Islam. However, the Orang Laut are aware of the possibility of choosing alternative religions which are also recognized by the Malays. They can thus decide to convert to Roman Catholicism, Protestantism, or *agama Tiong-hoa* (religion of the Chinese).[27] Those who select one of these alternatives perceive themselves as joining with the outside world through membership as believers in the faith (Wee, 1985:581).[28] On the one hand, they see other Orang Laut who do not have a religion as evil in comparison to themselves; at the same time they regard themselves as having formed an allegiance to a high centre more powerful than the Malays. They have, for example, told me about the leadership of the Pope and the powers of the Christian God.

As noted previously, the adoption of a religion signifies also transition from a nomadic to a sedentary lifestyle. For the Malays, this means that the Orang Laut have taken a step towards joining their community; however, from the perspective of the Orang Laut, this transition of their identity relocates them beyond the boundaries of the Malay World as an independent group. Certain aspects of the notion of purity are adopted for the purpose of making internal evaluations. I mentioned earlier that during the era of the Sultan, different groups of Orang Laut were ranked according to the task to which they were assigned. This system of classification from bygone days has deeply influenced the way in which different groups of Orang Laut view one another and, not surprisingly, each would rather identify itself with another more prestigious group.[29] They are constantly categorizing others as belonging to a less prestigious group even though the relation between work tasks and the prestige of a group is no longer relevant today.

There is, therefore, another ongoing idea of 'evilness or wickedness' that the Orang Laut capitalize on to demarcate internal divisions. It is the criterion of religion and language, as illustrated below by excerpts of two Orang Laut from two rival groups.

Suri:
We here are *Suku Galang*. Those on the opposite side are *Suku Barok*. Therefore, be careful of them. They speak *Bahasa Barok*. It is very funny when you listen to them. They reverse the meaning of words as

we would normally understand them. They cannot speak *Bahasa Melayu*. No one can comprehend them. The *Suku Barok* are evil. They are very powerful in their *ilmu* [*hitam*] (knowledge/[black] magic). They are not like us here. They are Catholics. We are Muslims and Protestants ... Catholics and Protestants are not the same. The Catholics are *orang lain* (different people/outsiders). They are evil. They do not pray like us.

Meen:
Did they tell you they were Suku Galang? They are lying. They make me laugh. They are ashamed to tell you they are Suku Tambus. They speak a different language from everyone else. Even I cannot understand their language. No one knows what they are talking about. I am Suku Barok and my wife is Suku Mantang. However, look at us here, we can speak Bahasa Melayu. The Suku Barok are good.

Be careful of those on the opposite side. They are very powerful in their *ilmu*. We have *ilmu* too, but we are not evil like the people on the opposite side. We are Catholics and do not want to poison anyone. They have no religion and enjoy poisoning people. They say that they are Muslims and Protestants. Nonetheless that is so only in name. They do not pray, and they still eat pork. We can eat pork because we are Catholics.

Suri and Meen are from Pulau Nanga and Teluk Nipah respectively. Their views adequately represent the opinions of the two communities. Both Suri and Meen have argued about group membership and the status accorded to different groups.[30] Proof for their non-evilness lies in their possessing a religion and their fluency in the Malay language. The excerpts above show Suri and Meen to be relating evilness and goodness to particular religious affiliations, as it is generally true that the Orang Laut of Teluk Nipah and Pulau Nanga see each other as evil because of their respective alignments to different religions. Still, it must be pointed out that the Orang Laut are aware that religious affiliation does not necessarily correspond to group membership. Those who identify themselves as *Suku Mantang* and *Suku Barok* on Teluk Nipah may claim allegiance to Roman Catholicism; yet they will also readily say that their *Suku Mantang* and *Suku Barok* siblings elsewhere are Muslims. They will explain that their relatives are real Muslims, hence not evil as compared to other Orang Laut neighbours on Pulau Nanga. The reason for this is that the Orang Laut of Pulau Nanga neither take their religion seriously nor adhere strictly to all the principles that have been laid down by the religion.

To sum up, the pure Malays see themselves as protectors of the Malay World. Those Orang Laut who refuse to be incorporated into this ordered world are seen as threatening, challenging, resisting, and endangering the ideal social structure. On the other hand, the Orang Laut have presented the pure Malays with an alternative worldview in which they make claims of power through indigenous status and *ilmu hitam*. The Malays disapprove of such sources of power, regarding them as impure and dangerous. There is, therefore, on the part of the Malays, a clear correlation between their authority and the control and dispensation of spiritual power (Leach, 1961; Douglas, 1985:101).

NOTES

1. See Wee (1985:118-66) and Wee and Chou (1997:528-32) for more details on the impact of each period on the Riau Archipelago.
2. The period of the Sultan commenced before 1511 and lasted for over 400 years.
3. The Republic of Indonesia was unilaterally declared by Sukarno on 17 August 1945 to be so, but officially achieved in 1949.
4. See Wee (1985:406-70) for a discussion on the hierarchies of being Malay in Riau. My field data correspond closely to her findings and analysis. I shall therefore only highlight issues which have not appeared in her analysis.
5. *Suku Barok* is also spelt *Suku Barut* and *Suku Bru* (Sopher, 1977:95).
6. See Sopher (1977) for a detailed description of the tasks assigned to the respective groups of Orang Laut.
7. The *Tuhfat al-Nafis* (The precious gift) is an official record of the history of Riau, authored by various members of the aristocracy. It is important to note how it stresses Penyengat's status as a centre of Islamic scholarship and an area governed by rulers who were devout Muslims (Matheson and Andaya, 1982; Matheson, 1989:164).
8. The Arabic *umma* means 'nation, people, generation' (Wehr, 1976:25).
9. See the *Tuhfat al-Nafis* (Raja Ali Haji ibn Ahmad, 1982), Raja Hamzah Yunus (1992), Wee (1985), and Matheson (1989) for documentation on the history of Penyengat.
10. See Endicott's (1991:91) discussion on how the beliefs in '*kramats*' [as spelt by Endicott] can influence events by revealing signs. Studies on the power these *keramat*s have also been dealt by Cuisinier (1936:32) and Annadale and Robinson (1904:24).
11. See Matheson (1989:159) and Wee (1985:324, 342) for a further discussion on these royal graves in Penyengat.

12 According to various written sources (Raja Ali Haji ibn Ahmad, 1982; Matheson, 1989) and the oral histories of my Malay informants, Raja Hamidah, who was also titled Engku Puteri (Raja Ali Haji, 1982:32), became the wife of Sultan Mahmud in 1804. Penyengat was her *mas kawin* (dowry). The Sultan gave instructions for 'the island to be cleared, and a royal residence with fortifications, a mosque, and an audience hall be constructed' (Matheson, 1989:159). My informants explain that it was thus Raja Hamida who opened up Riau, hence the need to seek her permission before journeying through it.

13 The Suku Oyol is another group of Orang Laut.

14 Both the Malays and Orang Laut from different areas in the Archipelago are known to have their own regional language and tribal dialects. Therefore, there is much dispute among the different groups of Malays and Orang Laut as to who is more refined or less coarse. According to Wee (1985), the Malays do not accept what the Orang Laut speak as a *bahasa* at all. However, contrary to her findings, I found it to be the case that my Malay and Orang Laut informants referred to the latter's speech as a *bahasa lain* (different language).

15 See Wee (1985:458-66) for a detailed discussion on how language is manipulated to indicate the purity of one's Malayness.

16 I cannot find any written records of a Panglima Ladi in Lingga. However, according to Sopher (1977:97), the *rakyat*s (populace, citizenry) of Lingga were under the leadership of a man called Panglima Raman. He is thought to have been a son of a Bugis trader and his mother is believed to have been the daughter of one of the leading citizens of that locality, probably belonging to the Suku Sekanak. As a youth, Raman had become a friend of the ruler, and later became one of his principal officers. Due to his maternal connection with the Orang Laut, he also became leader of the citizens, and was thus able to employ them in his master's political quarrels.

17 The names of these different *bangsa* of Orang Laut were spelt by Meen's son-in-law, Koeng. The latter had received three years of formal education.

18 The Orang Laut's description of one of their *Raja Laut* bears much similarity to 'one of the sea-people' identified as 'Badang' in The *Tuhfat* (Raja Ali Haji ibn Ahmad, 1982:13). Raja Ali Haji recorded that:

It was during the reign [of Raja Muda, who was entitled Seri Ratna Wikrama] that one of the sea-people, Badang, who was exceptionally strong, was able to uproot trees two or three spans wide because, it was said, he had eaten the vomit of a spirit.

19 The perception of Islam as entrenched in sedentism has led many Orang Laut to voice the following opinion,

Sara:
For those who are Muslims, they cannot live in the sea any longer. According to Islam, you cannot live in a boat. You cannot return to sea. You will be given a house on land. If you insist on living in the boat, your house will be taken away from you. As for those who have entered Christianity, we can still live in a boat. If you enter Islam and insist on returning to live in the boat, you will be jailed.

20 The Orang Laut are in a situation similar to that of the *Bajau Laut*, another group of non-Muslim sea-faring nomads in Indonesia. The *Bajau Laut* are believed to be spiritually cursed. Denied a place ashore, the *Bajau Laut* have been forced 'to live in boats, dispersed and looked down upon, without status or power' (Sather, 1984:13).

21 The Indonesian national ideology is to achieve *bhinneka tunggal ika* (unity in diversity) among the various groups of Indonesian peoples. An abstract creed known as *Pancasila* (Five Principles) prescribes belief in:

1. *Ketuhanan Yang Maha Esa* (A supreme Godhead).
2. *Kemanusiaan Yang Adil Dan Beradab* (A humanism that is legal and proper).
3. *Persatuan Indonesia* (The oneness of Indonesia).
4. *Kerakyatan Yang Dipimpim oleh Hikmah Kebijaksanaan Dalam Permusy Awararan/ Perwakilan* (A citizenry that is led by wise guidance through consultation/ representation).
5. *Keadilan Sosial Bagi Seluruh Rakyat Indonesia* (Social justice for all the Indonesian people).

I obtained a copy of this creed from the *Kantor Camat* (Subdistrict office) in Tanjung Pinang. The first principle implies that atheism is un-Indonesian. In this context, adherence to a religion is considered official proof that one is not a communist.

22 The *songkok* is worn by men when they pray and on formal occasions.
23 The representatives made this remark with reference to the fact that as they have adopted Islam, Bolong and Ceco are now also known as Muhammad and Ali.
24 Even when houses are built over the sea, people still urinate and defecate on land, rather than into the sea.
25 Scott (1985:171) explains *kenduri* as 'a sacred obligation' to 'promote social harmony' and to cleanse any 'jealousy or hatred' from all parties

concerned. It is usually an act of giving by the privileged to the less privileged. In the context of Islam, the benefactor, if of pure heart, will be rewarded. I share Scott's view (1985:169) that these *kenduri*s are 'sensitive barometers of class relations.' Therefore, they are 'rituals of compassion and social control.'

26 This Orang Laut woman had been baptized into Christianity by Christian missionaries. Christian missionaries had entered her husband's village while the couple were fishing together in the husband's village. On the other hand, the woman's brother was a Muslim as Muslim missionaries had persuaded his community to become Muslims.

27 Hinduism is an officially recognized religion too. However, my informants never talked of it as there were very few Hindus in the Riau Archipelago.

28 Roman Catholicism and Protestantism are two of the more popular alternative choices among the Orang Laut.

29 It was impossible to draw up a comprehensive list of the different groups of Orang Laut based upon information given by my informants. This was due to several problems. First, almost everyone would have a different listing. Second, it was not uncommon for them to make situational changes in their identity. Third, rival groups would often contradict each other on their identification claims. Wee (1985) was also confronted with the impossible task of deriving a comprehensive list from her informants. She (1985:245) offers the following explanation: 'whether this imposition of classificatory fragmentation had any effect on the indigens themselves would have depended on how previously they regarded the view of the political centre. The consequence is that it is practically impossible to obtain a comprehensive list of *suku*s because it all depends on who one asks.' This is a plausible reason. However, it can be conversely argued that the Orang Laut have been so influenced by the view of the former political centre that it pressurizes them to align themselves with a more prestigious group.

30 Based upon the hierarchical system of the former Sultanate, the *Suku Tambus* were regarded as 'being the lowest in rank. [They] had the meanest work, being in charge of the hunting dogs' (Sopher, 1977:93 quoted from Schot, 1882:472). In contrast, the *Suku Galang* were piratical sea nomads. Hence, they were accorded greater prestige because they could either align themselves with the power holders (Sopher, 1977:96-9) or pose potential threats to them (Wee, 1985:248).

CHAPTER 4

ILMU[1]

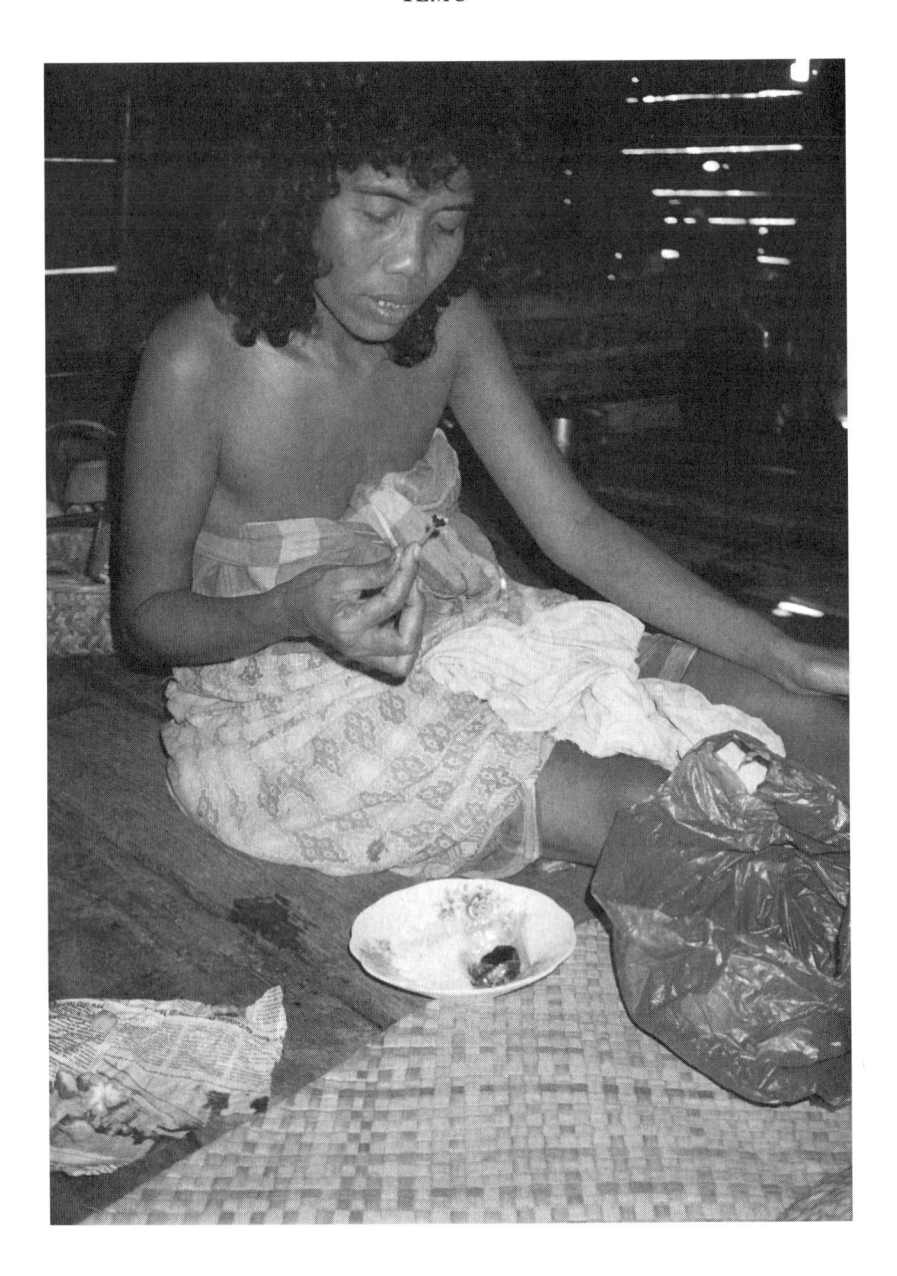

Picture 4: Casting a spell

The Malays often speak of the Orang Laut as possessing the most powerful *ilmu hitam*, more commonly referred to as *ilmu*, in the Malay World. This is believed to be a consequence of the Orang Laut's 'lack of religion.' The supernatural power is dangerous and *jahat* and can be exercised to bewitch innocent people. The greatest anxiety of the Malays and non-Malays alike is that they might be bewitched to *ikut* (follow) the Orang Laut into their lifestyle.[2] For the Malays, this would mean lapsing to the lowest rung of the Malay hierarchy.

The Orang Laut claim to possess the knowledge and ability to capture, subjugate, and harm the inner essence of others. The Malays see such powers as a constant challenge and threat to subvert the power structure of the ideal Malay World. In this chapter, I discuss the process by which the Orang Laut acquire this *ilmu*, and the methods and materials they use for abducting and controlling inner essences. This is essential in understanding how a person's inner essence can be merged with or embedded in things. As things can share a common identity with their owners, the meaning of a thing, its exchange, and the identity of the Orang Laut all come to be intertwined. The Orang Laut are also able to merge their being with spirits through practices of exchange and reciprocity.

SOURCES OF POWER

The Orang Laut are criticized by the Malays for having an 'uncertain' religion as they celebrate 'the festivals and religions of everyone.' They are not committed to the one God that Islam demands of its followers – an ambiguity which challenges the pure Malays' perception of Islam as the basis for legitimizing their leadership in the Malay World (Milner, 1981). The Malays are quick to point out that the Orang Laut are still beholden to spirits, and as a consequence, indulge in the evil pleasures of 'playing with poison' and 'harming' others. In contrast, the Orang Laut regard the Malays as evil because, they maintain, the Qur'an contains instructions on how to cast spells and practise black magic.[3] In fact, the Malays are said to be so evil that they are constantly trying to poison not only the Orang Laut but also other fellow Malays and even the Chinese. During the initial stages of my fieldwork, the Orang Laut were unwilling to divulge any information concerning their relationship with spirits. It was only well into the latter half of the first stretch of my fieldwork in 1992, when I had gained their trust, that they spoke of their associations with the *hantu laut* (sea spirits) and the *hantu darat* (land spirits).[4] Their initial denials stemmed from fears that I, like the Malays, would see them as 'evil.'

According to the Malays, good *ilmu* is revealed by God, while evil *ilmu* is derived from spirits.[5] The Orang Laut endorse such a general distinction, but think that spirits can render good *ilmu* as well. For the Orang Laut, any *ilmu* revealed by either God or spirits that can be used to 'help' the general well-being of a person is considered good *ilmu*.[6] They apply their *ilmu* in many areas of their life and are engaged in an on-going system of reciprocity with various spirits. Therefore, their achievements and successes are seen as testimonials to their relationship with these spirits and the resultant power of their *ilmu*.

This is clearly a situation where two systems of power clash within one society (Brown, 1970). On the one hand, the Malays define and agree that purity through Islam is the only recognized route to power in the Malay World.[7] No other source of power is accepted; all other 'impure, and hence polluting alternatives [of Malayness] are spurned' (Wee, 1985:550). Contrary to this is the Orang Laut's assertion of multiple sources of power. A tug of war thus ensues with each group accusing the other of practising evil *ilmu* and questioning the legitimacy of the other's power. What must be kept in mind is that accusations of *ilmu* serve an important social function for the Malays in structuring the hierarchy of power and domination in terms of what it means to be a 'pure' Malay in Riau.

ACQUIRING *ILMU*: THE INITIATION PROCESS

Evans-Pritchard (1976) distinguishes a 'witch' from a 'sorcerer': the witch possesses innate powers to harm others, while the sorcerer uses 'magic medicines' for similar results. Nevertheless, both sorcery and witchcraft have the same powers and they can be used to achieve good or evil deeds.

The Orang Laut and Malays refer to people who practise *ilmu* as *dukun*s and *bomoh*s (indigenous medicine people). These words are often interchangeable. However, sometimes, the two terms are used to differentiate between healers and other practitioners of *ilmu* (Endicott, 1991:13-14). The latter are usually described as people who *pakai ilmu* (use magic). Occasionally, my Orang Laut and Malay informants differentiate between the functions of magic and the methods of operations to harm others.[8]

The Malays believe that the Orang Laut are intrinsically evil and prone to practise evil *ilmu* to hurt others. However, I was not able to obtain clearly defined answers as to what constituted this intrinsic evilness. Neither were my Malay informants explicit in correlating this belief with any notion of hereditary witchcraft transmission. Instead, it was common to hear the Malays accusing the Orang Laut children of being evil because 'the children learn evil *ilmu* from their parents.' The Malays also talked about the Orang Laut acquiring their *ilmu* through their relationship with evil spirits. It seemed that neither the Orang Laut nor the Malays focused their attention on distinguishing hereditary magicians from initiated magicians. Their main concern revolved around the issue of whether it was the Orang Laut or the Malays who possessed and practised good or evil *ilmu*.

The Orang Laut are said to possess the most extensive *ilmu*, which enables them to diagnose and cure various illnesses, safeguard pregnancies and deliver babies, construct houses,[9] control the maritime world and winds,[10] hunt and gather jungle resources to supplement their diet,[11] pull in crowds when they entertain with their musical instruments during *joget* sessions, propitiate or intimidate spirits and control souls. Furthermore, the Orang Laut are always fearfully seen as concentrating their efforts upon preparing love potions to induct others into their way of life. While the Orang Laut acknowledge that they indeed possess the most powerful *ilmu* in the Malay World, they maintain that they only practise good *ilmu*. My Orang Laut informants have always stressed that they acquire their *ilmu* through formal training. The Orang Laut will form an attachment as a student or disciple to an established *dukun*. By going through a ceremony of initiation, the student will obtain the right to use the *ilmu* thus transmitted (Endicott, 1991:14).

Suri, an Orang Laut *dukun* renowned for her love charms and skills as a midwife, adopted me as a member of her family and initiated me into her *ilmu*. Suri had herself been initiated into the *ilmu* of her parents and various other *dukun*s. She was in the process of deciding which of her children should be initiated into her *ilmu* for delivering babies. She confided that her second youngest daughter, Anita, showed great potential. However, Suri feared that Anita was still too young to be initiated into such powerful *ilmu* as it could overpower her and lead to her death.

It was only towards the latter half of my fieldwork in 1992 that Suri trusted me enough to initiate me into her *ilmu*. I had expressed interest in acquiring a whole range of *ilmu* from controlling the maritime world to delivering babies. However, it was Suri who decided it was more important for me to be initiated into the various love charms. Like most of my Orang Laut friends, Suri was concerned because I was, at that time, still unmarried. She thought it most practical and important that I should deal with this matter immediately and decided that it would be best for me to learn how to 'beautify' myself to 'get any man' I desired and to 'protect' myself from any scorn.

The learning process stretched across a few months because Suri stipulated different conditions for the teaching and learning of different spells in order to ensure their effectiveness. For some spells to be effective,

Suri insisted that she could only impart her *ilmu* to me at certain times of the day. There were spells that could only be imparted while the sun was appearing or disappearing over the horizon. Other spells could not be uttered after mid-day or we would destroy the power in them. Furthermore, there were spells which Suri could repeat to me more than once during the teaching-learning process, while there were others which were impossible for her to repeat lest the spells lose their power. Suri initiated me into her *ilmu* in the utmost secrecy. I was taught to mumble or silently recite all the spells to maintain their secrecy. My mentor had to be certain that there was no one around to eavesdrop on our training sessions. I was told that this was to protect the power in our *ilmu*, but other Orang Laut *dukun*s explained that the eavesdropper would gain the power of the *ilmu,* and even worse, would be able to use the *ilmu* to harm the person who had originally possessed it. Apparently the Orang Laut believed that they could be harmed by others through their own *ilmu*. Throughout my training sessions with Suri, I was made to *sumpah* (swear) never to impart her *ilmu*[12] to anyone lest both of us be harmed. Her initiation of me into her *ilmu* meant that she had established a bond of common identity with me. Upon the completion of my sessions with Suri, she instructed me to present her with some tamarind, salt, and a nail. The nail was first dipped into the tamarind and salt before she licked part of it off. Suri then asked me to swallow the remainder of the salt and tamarind from the nail.

I was constantly reminded by my teacher that the incantation of a spell is incomplete without the manipulation of certain material objects. Sometimes, accompanying actions are also necessary to empower the spells. These accompanying materials and actions can be categorized according to their functions as 'boundary strengtheners,' 'boundary weakeners,' 'essence receptacles,' 'communicators' and 'offerings' for the persuasion of essences (or 'inner essences,' see below) (Endicott, 1991:133-45). The Orang Laut explain that whenever any spell is cast, both giver and recipient must respectively receive and give an iron nail, tamarind, and salt. This exchange is necessary to 'lock' the *ilmu* and ensures the continuing effectiveness of the *ilmu* when it is applied again at a later date. The powers of iron are well documented in the literature on Malay magic (Skeat, 1900; Winstedt, 1961; Swettenham, 1895). Iron is believed to function as a boundary strengthener (Endicott, 1991:133) in that it possesses the power to keep a person's soul in the body.[13] Thus, upon casting a spell, the giving of iron is to ensure that no vacuum is left for other spirits to enter. Iron maintains the boundaries of the body and the environment.

Upon the conclusion of my training sessions, Suri also reminded me to give her some money along with a non-monetary item.[14] *Ilmu* is an inalienable possession of the Orang Laut. Therefore, Suri stressed that she could not ask for money nor quote a specific amount as that would mean that she was selling her *ilmu*. She emphasized that the money that I would 'give' her was not similar to paying for something that I had bought. This was because she was neither keen nor able to sell her *ilmu*. Rather, Suri maintained that she had chosen to impart her *ilmu* to me and not to anyone else, as *ilmu* was not something that could be circulated freely.

Initiation ceremonies prominently involve a payment by the initiate to the living teacher in the line of transmission. The ceremony marks the incorporation of the initiate into a particular magical tradition. The initiate also swears to secrecy the *ilmu* of that particular tradition. This is a condition for the initiate to gain the right to use the *ilmu*. All initiates are taught that spells must be protected, and that spells can only be silently recited or mumbled. Prospective magicians may study with more than one master, and the teacher could be one's parent, relative, or even someone from outside the community (Endicott, 1991:14-15). The items that Suri had asked for therefore constituted a form of exchange to indicate that I was entering into a line of transmission in a particular magical tradition. The 'initiation creates artificially a right to use *ilmu* analogous to the right transmitted naturally by heredity' (Endicott, 1991:15; Cuisinier, 1936:7).

People who practise *ilmu* do all they can to maintain the secrecy surrounding their *ilmu* in order to safeguard its effectiveness. It is also professional jealousy that causes *ilmu* to be so closely guarded. *Dukun*s need to know what other people do not know, and sharing their knowledge would diminish their importance and the demand for their services. It is precisely because *ilmu* is believed to work for anyone that it is jealously guarded (Endicott, 1991:19-20). To understand the full implications of *ilmu*, it is also necessary to understand that *ilmu* is an inalienable possession that bears a common identity with its owner. As an inalienable possession, it can only be passed down or given under certain conditions, hence the initiation ceremony with its attached conditions. Owners must guard their possessions well as they may be harmed via their inalienable possessions which bear a common identity with them.

THE INNER ESSENCE

The Orang Laut maintain that *ilmu* controls every aspect of life. Central to the whole system of *ilmu* is the belief in *semangat* and *ruh* or what can be translated as 'soul substance' (Endicott, 1991:53). I use this term to encompass the concept of an Orang Laut's soul or inner essence and power.

In analysing Malay magic, Endicott (1991:48) talks about three distinct types of soul: *semangat*, *nyawa*, and *roh* (or *ruh*). He argues that the *semangat, nyawa,* and *roh* can be understood as different aspects of the single human soul which, he states, is usually referred to as the *semangat.* That is to say, s*emangat* in its undifferentiated state can therefore mean all three collectively.

I observed that the Orang Laut often used the term '*semangat*' in their spells, but changed to the word '*roh*' when talking about the souls of deceased persons. Beyond this, they were never clear in making a distinction between the two terms. Their concern was to explain how the inner essence of a person could be appeased or attacked. Following their practice, I will use the terms in a broad sense to mean the inner essence and power of the Orang Laut.

The conversations that I have had with the Orang Laut indicate that the soul may or may not be attached to the body of a person. Upon Siti's death, her relatives explained how the deceased Siti was still present in the form of her *roh* in the Pulau Nanga community. Although Siti's *roh* was not embedded in a body to make its presence visible, her sister-in-law Suri explained that it is common for the *roh* to appear in the form of a *hantu* (spirit/ ghost).

> Suri:
> Siti will roam around Pulau Nanga for a hundred days after her death. We have to hold *kenduri*s for her until the hundredth day. You may think that you cannot see Siti. In any case, if you did, you would die of shock too! However, each time we hold a *kenduri* for Siti, her *roh* is hovering above us. We cannot see Siti, but her *roh* can see what we are doing and is satisfied. When we *jampi* (cast a spell on) the food over the burning incense during the *kenduri*, we are inviting Siti to eat and not harm us. The smoke from the burning incense shows that Siti is eating the food. When the smoke dies down, it indicates that Siti is full. It is only after that that we can eat. However, the food will lack taste because Siti has consumed all the essence of the food. After a hundred days, it will not be necessary for us to hold any more *kenduri*s for Siti. After that, we will only have a *kenduri* for Siti when she appears in our dreams. These dreams will be an indication that Siti is hungry. We will have to appease her by holding another *kenduri*.

The Orang Laut use *kenduri*s or food offerings to persuade or appease souls. The type of food offered varies. Usually, these offerings are things that people themselves desire and eat (Endicott, 1991:142-3). The Orang Laut also believe that the smoke and smell of the incense which fumigates the offerings can penetrate space and certain boundaries in the physical world to capture the attention of essences.[15] This paves the way for them to establish contact and communication with essences (Endicott, 1991:140).

> Suri:
> I dream of the *roh* of the person. It appears as a spirit in my dreams. When I dream of the spirit, the dream always occurs at about five or six in the morning. I am able to wake up and still be conscious of my dream. It is an *asli* (authentic) dream; the face of the spirit will appear. If I did not see the face of the spirit, then I would not be brave enough. The dream would be from Satan disturbing us ... we must not do anything.
>
> If a person dies properly, the person's *roh* and face will appear to us in our dreams to implore us properly for food. I dreamt of my mother asking for chicken when my sister-in-law Ross was ill ... You must not fool around. When a spirit appears in your dreams, you will wake up and see it. I was sleeping and it approached me and said, 'Wake up! Wake up!' I already saw the face of the spirit in my dreams while I was asleep. I woke up and exclaimed, 'Ah, what is it?' The spirit said, 'There is someone who wants to approach you.' I replied, 'Who's that?' It replied, 'Your mother.' The spirit woke me up.
>
> When my mother had just died, I fell ill and she appeared three times in my dreams. She said, 'Ask your husband to prepare medicine from leaves and wood.' I asked, 'What sort of medicine?' She said, 'For you to get well.'

From these excerpts of conversations, it is clear that the inner essence and power of a person constitute the 'identity' and 'symbol' of the person's existence even after death (Endicott, 1991:31).

SPELLS

I present a few samples of spells here. These spells appear in translation form, i.e., not in the original language in which I was trained. I am under oath not to disclose the original words to anyone.

The use of spells to attack a person is really an attack on their inner being rather than a direct attack on their physical body. Spells can therefore work in various ways. In love spells (1), (4), and (5) which appear below, Suri, the *dukun* who initiated me into her *ilmu*, explained that these are spells meant to charm a person into falling in love with me. Endicott (1991:50) has pointed out that such spells aim at controlling the soul without weakening or extracting it. On the other hand, love spells (2) and (3) are so powerful that they could be used to drive a person who has criticized me for lack of beauty into surges of passion leading to his insanity and suicide. This correlates with Endicott's (*ibid*:50-1) analysis that some spells work through the abduction of a person's soul driving him into madness, rather than love. This sort of spell 'represents the revenge of a shunned suitor [rather] than true love charms' (*ibid*:51). Such a spell works by extracting the soul of the victim, leaving the victim's body out of control. The victim may become ill and even die, as the absence of the soul renders the body vulnerable to the entry of evil spirits. The symptoms are loss of memory, confused speech, and failure to recognize even one's own parents. While there is a dependence of the body on the soul, it is also possible for the soul and the body to be separated. This would not result in the soul being displaced. It simply means that the soul can enter and leave the body of its owner in certain circumstances. For this reason, the Orang Laut believe that they can share a common identity with a person's possessions. The inner essence of a person is able to cross boundaries to merge with another person or to be embedded in things. This is why both the Orang Laut and the Malays believe that their inner being can be harmed via their body or through things that share a common identity with them.[16] To accept something from someone else is, then, to accept (part of) the soul of the other. The incantation of spells with the manipulation of material objects therefore makes it possible for the Orang Laut to control, abduct, and subjugate others via their inner essences, as illustrated in the following spells.

1.
In the name of God, may the struggling betel nut be split![17]
Come hither, be split above the rock!
In whichever way your *hati* (heart/liver/mind) spins.
Let it bend to me!
Semangat of my lover return to me!
Semangat of mine be one with yours!

2.
Sweet lime in the moon
Upon the wishing moon, sit and cry!
Reveal and submit yourself to me.
I turn your *semangat* towards me!
Return!
Your *semangat* return to me!
My *semangat* be one with yours!

Forlorn young hawk[18]
Come hither, remember your awaiting death.
Anxiety plague you as you sit and as you stand.
Reveal and submit yourself to me because I command you under hypnosis.
May the face in the mirror be a reflection
To be loved.
May this face that you see in this mirror
Be the only one upon whom you will lock your gaze fixedly for being the prettiest of all!

Young bird, come towards
The face in the mirror that is reflected beyond.
Let your *hati* be one with mine
Bending to my commands
In the name of God!

Forlorn young hawk, come towards the mirror!
Hither, with throbbing pains in your lowered head and swaying with death under the direct heat of the sun!
With the yearnings of a newborn baby
Be plagued with anxiety as you sit and as you stand!
Because I command your *hati* to be feeble.

In the love spells above, there are explicit utterances of *semangat* to indicate the working of the love spells by soul abduction. Although it is common for the word '*semangat*' to appear in love spells, not all make such direct reference to capturing the soul. This is seen in the sample below.

3.
Stormy day
Thrust yourself towards the sea
Row towards the island!

Leave me a piece of cloth torn from you
To capture and excite your serene *hati*.

Stormy heart thrust towards the island
In loneliness go towards and fall into the foul salt water.

Live to be ridiculed for my pleasure

To see [it all as] a story in comic form!
4.
In the name of God, wishing upon the sweet horizoned moon![19]
Hither, be served upon a wooden platter
Upon the wishing moon, cry lover!
In the name of God, wishing upon the sweet horizoned moon
Cry as you sit, stoop in submission to me!

5.
In the name of God, let the *ribu-ribu* (an ivy-like creeping vine) cover your path!
The young crocodile is clearly doubtful
Allowing a thousand friends to pass!
His love to be given to me alone
I am the prettiest of them all.

Although no direct reference was made to abducting the *semangat,* these spells share some general features. They all contain pleas, commands, or threats which are meant to persuade or coerce the inner essence of another person into total submission to the magician.

Mere incantation of the spells is insufficient. I was instructed by the *dukun* to cast, first of all, the love spells that I had been taught onto limes. The limes were then to be immersed in the water in which I was to bathe. Afterwards, the pulp of the limes would be thrown away.

In casting love spells, it is vital that boundaries of bodies be weakened to admit the passage of essences from one person to another. Water is important for weakening boundaries, because it is fluid. It cannot sustain divisions or boundaries (Endicott, 1991:136). The mention of water in love spells and the accompanying act of bathing together enable the essences to cross boundaries in order to be merged. Limes, pieces of cloth, and leaves are also commonly referred to and used as receptacles or substitute bodies for absorbing essences (Endicott, 1991:139). By casting the love spells into limes, one's essence is enticed into the limes which then act as receptacles when abducting other souls. Also, the distasteful acidity of the lime fruit is thought to incapacitate spirits so that they can be controlled once they have been absorbed (*ibid*:138-40). Sometimes a piece of 'cloth,' as uttered in the third love spell, is used in ways similar to limes.[20] Skeat (1900:51) calls it a 'soul cloth' when it is used to retrieve or abduct a soul. In the third spell, mention is also made of *ribu-ribu* (a kind of creeper). Brushes made of grass or leaves tied together with *ribu-ribu* or a string of *daun t'rap* (shredded tree bark) are yet other kinds of essence receptacles to absorb and subdue essences for disposal (Endicott, 1991:136-40). Clearly the Orang Laut make use of all known ways in casting spells for the purpose of controlling, abducting, and subjugating others.

FISHING AND CIRCULATION OF FOOD WITH SEA SPIRITS

The Orang Laut believe they depend on the *hantu laut* (sea spirits) for the safety and success of all their maritime activities. In ways similar to the manner in which they lure the soul of a person towards them through love spells, they communicate with the spirit of their prey. It is also often the case that the Orang Laut will establish communication with the spirits in charge of their environment. There are variations in the manner in which different Orang Laut communities present their pleas and offerings to the sea spirits, although some general basic beliefs underlie all. The Orang Laut maintain that 'everyone including the Westerners' know about spirits, such as the sea spirits, and the only difference is that others may or may not be willing to talk about their relationship with the spirits.

The Orang Laut assert that there is a *Raja Hantu Laut* (King Sea Spirit) who reigns over the entire maritime world, as well as a female sea spirit who is 'Mother' to all things. The *Raja* and Mother Sea Spirits have their *anak buah* (follower) sea spirits, who are sometimes referred to as *anak hantu laut* (child sea spirits). The Orang Laut liken these child sea spirits to children of human beings who are constantly up to mischief.

As the sea spirits are seen as owning and controlling everything in the maritime world, the Orang Laut believe the relation between the maritime world and the human world must be mediated through an exchange with the spirits. They explain that things in the maritime world are not simply caught and killed. Rather, it is the sea spirits who withhold or release things in the maritime world and allow these things to offer themselves to pursuing humans.[21] The Orang Laut thus deem it necessary to establish a spiritual link with the maritime world in their fishing activities. They confess that they are not able to communicate verbally with the sea spirits, but stress the importance of casting spells to persuade the fish to yield themselves. Below is an example of such a spell.

> Darting obstructions
> Come hither!
> Come in from the right, come in from the left!
> May all the fish be sucked into the centre of the water!

This spell shows that the Orang Laut believe they are able, through the sea spirits, to control the water and weather conditions to help them carry out their fishing activities effectively. They also maintain that all fishing equipment used at sea comes immediately under the authority of the sea spirits. The sea spirits are basically 'satan,' hence 'evil,' but the Orang Laut claim it is possible for sea spirits to do evil or good depending on how well they themselves *piara* (adopt and feed) the spirits.[22] If they adopt/feed them well, the spirits 'like to help' them. By the same token, they adopt/feed the sea spirits well in order to obtain knowledge of the sea for a good catch. To neglect or offend the sea spirits would result in the sea spirits 'stealing' from human beings or even doing something fatal. One Orang Laut explains:

Ceco:
[If the sea spirits are not well fed], we will fall ill. We will suffer from dizziness. We will vomit immediately and our face will turn yellow. These are the symptoms of someone who has been harmed by the sea spirits. What we will have to do then is to go to the spirit's place to see if we have made an offering. If not, we have to cast spells to say that we are good and not bad. We will have to plead with the sea spirits not to harm us. If we do not do this, we will be harmed because the spirits own the territory.

If the sea spirits are angered, they will invade and devour the inner essence of people. Therefore, the Orang Laut offer the sea spirits anything they ask for. If the spirits do not make a specific request, then 'all sorts of food,' including whole chickens and rice, are offered. It is said that entire villages stand in danger of being wiped out if one forgets to feed the sea spirits.

The spirits communicate their desire for food through dreams. Dreams are an important channel of communication between hunters in the human world and the animal world and provide the hunters with a partial insight into their ongoing and future productive activities. As such insights reflect the hunters' communication with the animal world, dreams bespeak a person's potential spiritual power (Tanner, 1979:126-7). In ways similar to the hunters, the Orang Laut interpret their dreams as a union with the maritime world. Their ability to harvest a good catch or bigger varieties, such as turtles and crocodiles from the sea and mangrove swamps, is seen as indicative of their spiritual power. The Orang Laut of Pulau Nanga often boasted to me about the magical powers of their eldest brother Bolong, who is also the Headman of the Orang Laut community of Pulau Nanga. They explained that encounters with crocodiles were not only dangerous, but possibly fatal too. However, whenever Bolong worked in partnership with his first wife, he was able to cast spells on the crocodiles at the end of his harpoon and persuade them to give up their struggle and come to him instead.[23]

Sea spirits may be visible or invisible. The Orang Laut say that if they are fortunate, they might meet a sea spirit by chance. On such occasions, they will approach with the plea, 'Do not harm me, and I will not harm you. I am looking for fish, just as you are looking for food.'[24] Some Orang Laut report that if they feel 'cold,' they are potentially able to see the sea spirits. Sea spirits are said to resemble human beings in some respects, such as possessing hair and teeth. It is, however, possible to distinguish them from human beings because they are always exceptionally good looking, but with blood-shot eyes. The spirits also possess a very white and fair complexion. The Orang Laut were constantly telling me that ghost stories on television only confirmed the existence and authenticity of spirits such as the sea spirits.

Before embarking on a fishing trip, the Orang Laut will ask the sea spirits for *ilmu*. They will plead with the spirits to grant their request by offering fish in front of their boats. This is followed with a promise to feed the spirits, should their request be granted. The sea spirits are then said to enter the inner being of the fisherman. Spells are also cast in order to gain spiritual linkage with the sea spirits who may then allow the fish to come to the surface to be speared. It is understood that all good catches are due to the sea spirits' help and, conversely, all poor catches are the direct result of their unwillingness.

After each successful catch, the Orang Laut must cast spells again and offer cigarettes and *pulot* (glutinous rice) to the sea spirits. In addition, they must bathe from head to toe lest the spirits devour their souls. An offering could be as simple as a plate of *pulot puteh* (white glutinous rice), an egg, and some cigarettes. Some throw the offerings into the sea; others carefully place their offerings on rocks jutting out into the sea. All dangerous rocks are believed to be the 'homes' of sea spirits. Once offerings have been made to the sea spirits to acknowledge their help, the food and other things are consumed by the people. Afterwards, the recipients must bathe and cast spells to get the spirits out of their bodies. Below is an example of a spell to *buang hantu laut* (throw away the sea spirits):

Hacking the betel nut
Casting into half the rolling betel nut
Let the sea come in like the wind
May the sea spirit(s) be forced out without a fight!

Failure to bathe and cast such a spell may cause the spirits to 'eat' the person. The use of water and bathing in conjunction with spells functions as a boundary weakener, facilitating the exit of the sea spirits from one's inner being.

Fishing, the main preoccupation and occupation of the Orang Laut, is thus an exchange between the maritime world and the human world. Exchange and reciprocity connect the two worlds. The use of cash for such exchanges is inappropriate because, as will be discussed in Chapter 7, cash has the function of putting distance into the relationship between transactors. For the Orang Laut, this transaction is not within a society with its hierarchical organization, but between the human society and the forces upon which it must draw (Gudeman, 1986:148-50).

The beliefs of the Orang Laut contradict the principles of Islam as propagated by the pure Malays, who often speak of dangerous and fearsome evil spirits in association with such observances.[25] My Orang Laut informants told me that even before their adoption of any religion, they had always believed in the existence of a higher God. They maintain that although they are presently encouraged to take up a 'religion,' it is still their conviction that 'all religions lead to the same God.' This, of course, directly contradicts the notion of a single path to purity upheld by the Malays. The Orang Laut believe in the idea of a single unitary essence which was diffused throughout creation. Alternatively put, they believe that beneath the apparent diversity of things is a cosmic unity which is God. Parallel to this belief is the understanding that all spirits pervading the whole world, even if they are known by different names, are really one (Endicott, 1991:43-5).[26] For the Orang Laut, the multiplicity of spirits, whether good or evil, is merely so in appearance. This understanding of a single unitary essence in the multiplicity of spirits can also be extended to include the Orang Laut's notion of the inner essence or soul of a person. Once again, they believe that all things, whether knowledge or objects, are able to bear a common identity with their owner. This is because people's inner essence can be diffused into their possessions.

The Orang Laut are therefore seen as having the ability to merge their being with all spirits and things. This means that the Orang Laut are accused of practising witchcraft, which gives them a particular spiritual authority to control events, things, and other people. For the Malays, this implies that the Orang Laut have the power to harm others and subvert all forms of order.

WITCHCRAFT, SUSPICION, AND THE SOCIAL ORDER

The framework provided by Douglas's theory of witchcraft (1970:xxvi-xxvii) is very helpful in understanding the situation here. She differentiates two types of witchcraft: the witch as outsider and the witch as internal enemy. The internal witch is further distinguished into three sub-types: the witch as a member of a rival faction, the witch as a dangerous deviant, and the witch as an internal enemy with outside connections.

My Orang Laut and Malay informants' views of each other correlate quite closely to Douglas's characterization of the witch as an internal enemy belonging to a rival faction. The Malays, especially those who claim to be pure Malays, embrace a centralized, concrete, homogenous, immutable, and all-encompassing power structure under Islam and, out of their fear of being challenged, go so far as to assert the notion of a 'Single Image' (Brown, 1970:22) of power which can only be legitimized by Islamic principles.[27] The Orang Laut, though acknowledged as indigenous Malays, profess allegiance to different religious beliefs and practise their *ilmu*. This religious ambivalence or diffusion and the power they gain from their *ilmu* combine to present an alternative form of Malayness. They are, therefore, regarded as witches or betrayers of a close community, capable of promoting factional rivalry, splitting community, and redefining hierarchy (Douglas, 1970). In short, they poison and subvert the social order.

The accusations of evil *ilmu* are only directed at those who perceive themselves as belonging to the Malay World. It is well known that witches and their accusers are usually people belonging to the same community (Marwick, 1990; Douglas, 1970) and, nearly always, the accusations stem either from personal hostilities (Mayer, 1990:62) or from areas where unresolvable tensions exist between people in ambiguous social relations (Douglas, 1970:xvi-xvii). These are also the causes for accusations of evil *ilmu* in Riau. Both the Orang Laut and Malays believe that non-Malays such as the Chinese are not capable of witchcraft, even though they may be harmed and poisoned by *ilmu*.

The witch is, furthermore, identified as 'an attacker and deceiver' (Douglas, 1970:xxvi) who explicitly and triumphantly challenges the state of society that is 'desired and thought "good"' (Nadel, 1990:298). He uses what is 'impure and potent to harm what is pure and helpless. The symbols of what we recognize across the globe as witchcraft all build on the theme of vulnerable internal goodness attacked by external power' (Douglas 1970:xxvi). Efforts, then, must be made to neutralize these enemies of society. Therefore, the pure Malays are particularly keen to recruit the Orang Laut into their way of life (Wee, 1985:540). Different means, considered not to conflict with the perceived ideals of society, are employed for this purpose. The push to enter Islam and follow a sedentary lifestyle is but one of the ways to reintegrate those held to be practitioners of evil *ilmu* into the wider Malay community. However, the Orang Laut have not responded in the manner desired, and more importantly, have represented a viable alternative to being Malay. Therefore, accusations and counter-accusations, pressure and resistance have all become constant fare in Riau not only as ways of stressing the relative purity and goodness of one or the other group (Wee, 1985:540) but, even more importantly, as efforts in disguise of asserting the limits in the hierarchy of power and authority.

Accusations of evil *ilmu* thus enable the Malay World in Riau, which is fraught with unresolvable conflicts and contradictions, to continue to function in an acceptable manner. They have allowed the Malays and the Orang Laut to conceal their hostilities. Such accusations enable people to reprove those whom they consider personally distasteful in ways which cannot be expressed openly (Wyllie, 1990:132-9) through physical or legal means (Mayer, 1990:62). The Malays see the need to bring evilness under human control in order to uphold a particular moral order (Krige, 1990:263). But, in ways similar to witchcraft beliefs, accusations of evil *ilmu* free society from the difficult task of 'radical readjustment' (Nadel, 1990:299). In fact, they act as catalysts in the process of segmentation in the perceived hierarchy of 'pure' and 'impure' Malays in Riau. In accusing someone of evil *ilmu*, punishments of an appropriate sort may be meted out to the agents of evil, such as the Orang Laut, to alleviate the frustrations suffered by the believers, in this case the self-defined pure Malays. What must also not be overlooked is the fact that the champions of the ideal society always attempt to dismiss the possibility that frustrations may also arise from submitting to the social ideal (Nadel, 1990:298).

NOTES

1. The word '*ilmu*' is an Arabic-derived word which means 'knowledge' or science. Wilkinson (1959:421) lists the different kinds of 'knowledge' that the word '*ilmu*' refers to as 'learning [based on divine revelation], science, magic, any branch of knowledge or magic.' According to Endicott (1991:13), the Malay word for magic is *ilmu*. Thus, the term used by the Orang Laut and Malays can be translated as magic, witchcraft and/or knowledge derived from a spiritual realm. I am using the word interchangeably to refer to any one of these aspects.
2. Although most of the Chinese in Riau are not Muslims, they are regarded as a safe people with their own 'Chinese religion.'
3. According to Endicott (1991:15), 'another way to obtain *ilmu* is through *tuntut* (pursuing knowledge), seeking after it by practices such as praying, fasting, and reciting the Qur'an until a revelation comes in a dream or a spell of temporary madness.'
4. The sea spirits and land spirits are not to be confused with the spirits of deceased people.

5 The Malays believe that Muslim Malay *bomoh*s or *dukun*s (practitioners of indigenous medicine) possess good *ilmu*. Such healers claim that they only use Qur'anic verses to cast their spells. They claim to practise *ilmu sihir* which is supposed to be derived from Islam, even though it is not part of Islam as such (Wee, 1985:531). The Arabic word, *sihir*, does indeed mean 'bewitchment, beguilement, enchantment, fascination ... sorcery, witchcraft, magic, charm (of a woman)' (Wehr, 1976:400).

6 The Orang Laut and Malays believe that there also exists neutral knowledge such as scientific knowledge (Wee, 1985:530), which is derived from outsiders. The *ilmu* that a person possesses is used to prepare either good and safe, or bad and dangerous *obat* (medicines). 'Foreign' or 'western' medicines are considered safe because they are prepared from neutral knowledge. My informants know that these medicines are 'powerful' and overdoses may prove fatal. However, such deaths are viewed differently from being 'poisoned' by someone's black magic. The Orang Laut explain that medicine prepared by good and evil *ilmu*, unlike 'western medicine,' is made of 'leaves and wood.' Hence, they are cautious of people with such capabilities. The Orang Laut stress that the only other people apart from themselves who prepare such medicines in Riau are the Malays. The Chinese are not seen as possessing such *ilmu*. According to the Orang Laut, Chinese physicians are the only Chinese with the potential to poison anyone. This is because they possess extensive knowledge of 'making medicine from leaves and wood.' However, the Orang Laut are certain that Chinese physicians, unlike the Malays, have no interest in poisoning anyone.

7 This is especially so with the pure Malays who are the power holders in the Malay World.

8 However, Endicott (1991:13-19) maintains that the Malays make distinctions between hereditary and initiated magicians. He notes that the magic of hereditary magicians is considered more effective. Wee (1985:531) also sees the applicability of Evans-Pritchard's definition of witches and sorcerers in Riau. She (Wee, 1985:531-2) proposes the following explanation:

... a Muslim [Malay] is regarded as intrinsically good, whereas a non-Muslim [Malay] is regarded as intrinsically bad. As a consequence, [it is believed that] only the good can have good 'knowledge'; the bad would have access only to bad 'knowledge' ... I have glossed this bad 'knowledge' as 'witchcraft' because evil is attributed not to the act of knowing, but to the person who knows ... The *bomoh* (shaman) ... exists even in the communities that are considered [pure] ... The kind of 'knowledge' that a *bomoh* has is generally referred to as *ilmu sihir* ...

The 'knowledge' of such sorcerers is considered acceptable if these sorcerers are themselves as acceptable as Muslims ... *Ilmu sihir* is thus supposed to have an Islamic derivation ... Because of this ..., a *bomoh*'s *ilmu sihir* is not regarded as intrinsically evil ... In contrast, the bad 'knowledge' of witchcraft is an evil mystery to which my [pure] informants feel they have no direct access.

9   The use of *ilmu* is deemed necessary for choosing the best site and time for the building process. It is also necessary in the process of adopting a house.
10 Control of the winds is especially important for navigational purposes. Also, winds send ripples across the surface of the sea. This makes it difficult for the Orang Laut to gauge the position of the fish for their spear-fishing method.
11 It is believed that *ilmu* is necessary for attracting one's prey, making equipment (traps, snares, etc.) effective, and for protection against any dangers in the carcasses of the animals killed. It is also believed that *ilmu* is necessary for the gathering of jungle resources to propitiate the spirits that guard the products (Endicott, 1991:24).
12 This differs from Endicott's (1991) analysis of Malay magic, in that he only discusses *ilmu* as 'magical knowledge' without seeing it as having the capacity to contain the soul substance of its possessor.
13 Other elements such as gold and silver are also believed to possess similar powers to iron. However, because of their scarcity and costliness, substitutes are used. For example, white cotton thread is used to represent silver. In Chapter 7, I describe the giving of a white cotton thread to a midwife after she had applied her *ilmu* on a conceiving woman. The Orang Laut also use tumeric to dye the rice that is used to offer to spirits. The colour yellow, I believe, is a colour association to represent gold. The scattering of yellow rice to spirits is used in different situations. For instance, when I was in the Orang Laut community in Tiang Wang Kang, a pregnant woman developed premature pains. A *dukun* prepared a plate of variously coloured rice – yellow being one of the colours – laid out in the shape of a human being. The *dukun* rotated the plate over the head of the woman and simultaneously cast a spell. I was told that this was to protect the other surviving members of the community.
14 The role of money will be further discussed in Chapter 7.
15 Lighted candles also serve the same function. In Chapter 7, I describe how an Orang Laut midwife upon the completion of her services is given a lighted candle stuck into a coconut. In turn, the coconut is pierced with a needle and white cotton thread. I have already explained the

significance of the white cotton thread. The needle, which has the quality of sharpness, is to ensure continued perfect eyesight for the mid-wife to carry on in her skills. The coconut, with its quality of hardness, is to strengthen boundaries. The lighted candle which is placed with all these things purports to invite and guide the spirits to enter the candles when they appear on the scene. The flickering and flaring up of the flame are signs that there is disturbance in the air because of the arrival of the spirit that has indeed entered the candle (Endicott, 1991:141).

16 This spiritual bond between owners and their things bears some similarity to Mauss's (1990) description of Maori things. Mauss relates how things are tied into their owner's nature and substance.

17 The betel nut is a metaphor and/or conception of the soul (Endicott, 1991: 135).

18 According to Endicott (1991:80), who draws his analysis from Skeat (1900:47), the bird is a common Indonesian conception of the soul. As such, references are made about the soul being detached from the body and flying away (*ibid*:139).

19 According to Malay belief, it is a propitious time when the moon appears over the horizon.

20 According to Endicott (1991:139), cloths hold such powers because 'cloths recall the shrouds so prominent in imagery of ghosts and may represent the constraint of the grave to spirits that have escaped it.'

21 Parallels can be drawn with other hunting communities who, like the Orang Laut, directly interact with and exploit the natural resources in their surrounding environment. Tanner's (1979) and Bodenhorn's (1988, 1989, 1990) work, among the Mistassini Cree Indian hunters and the Alaskan North Slope Inupiat hunters respectively, are examples of how hunting is 'a sacred act' (Bodernhorn, 1990:61) encompassing a whole set of 'technical' and 'symbolic' activities (*ibid*:55) which celebrate the 'spiritual connection between humans and animals' (*ibid*:64). The Inupiat make and wear specially designed hunting garments which combine 'social,' 'spiritual' and 'technological elements' (Chaussonnet, 1988:210) to 'spiritually' link 'animals, hunters and seamstresses together in an intricate and circular set of relationships' (*ibid*:212).

22 The word '*piara*' will be discussed in greater detail in the following chapter.

23 The Orang Laut consider a marriage good or a couple well suited for one another if together in a working partnership, they are able to bring in good catches (Chou 1995:185).

24 The Orang Laut explained that they would feed spirits with types of food, such as glutinous rice and eggs, that are also eaten by human beings. I was also told that angry or hungry spirits would devour the

inner essence of human beings. However, I remain uncertain as to whether or not fish and other maritime products form part of the sea spirits' diet.

25 Tanner (1979:198) has similar accounts of the Cree Indian hunters' practices running contrary to the Christian morality upheld by the wider community. Although the hunters have absorbed some Christian elements into their practices, those belonging to the wider community still associate the Christian concept of the devil with the practices of the Cree Indians. This can once again be compared to the situation of the Orang Laut.

26 This is comparable to the Negrito Batek De's concept of deities. The deities of the Batek De are unique and yet clearly related to the deities of all the other Negrito groups. This is because there is an underlying unity in the multiplicity of deities. Rhyming names are given to these deities to denote the various shifting roles that they assume. Yet, these rhyming names also put into perspective the basic image of a single all-encompassing deity of the Negritos (Endicott, 1979).

27 This polarization of good and evil is compounded by Indonesian state policies which state that those who do not profess any of the recognized religions are considered communists.

Chapter 5

The Meaning of Things:
Constructions of the Orang Laut's Identity

Picture 5: Constructing a *serampang*, a fishing spear

This chapter is about the objectification of identity, i.e., the modes in which artefacts and skills signify individual or collective identities (Miller, 1987). There is, so to speak, 'a one-to-one relationship between a material thing (or a particular array...) and the expression of belonging to or difference' from a particular person or group (Thomas, 1991:25). That is to say, 'the object may lend itself equally to the expression of difference ... and to the expression of unity' (Miller, 1987:130). I will show below how the choice or avoidance of different types of objects in the Malay World signifies cultural contrasts and social alternatives.

'Exchange relations' in the Malay World, to a large extent, constitute 'the substance of social life' (Thomas, 1991:7). Something as simple as the movement of an object is not merely a physical process. It is also an entanglement of transactors in wider and deeply entrenched social relations, and a jostle among them in order to ascertain the appropriate transaction forms for upholding the perceived social order. As articulated by Thomas (1991:19), a thing 'is not simply... [an] object of exchange or even a gift that creates relations of one sort or another, but also a crucial index of the extent to which those relations are sustained or disfigured. The failure to recognize the distinctions that artefacts stand for suggests a succession of other failures 'to the extent that recognition of meaning is withheld from the sign ... so too it [the object as a sign] is withheld from the relationships and bonds that it is supposed to signify' (Tanner, 1979:340).

In any given transaction, the Orang Laut and their Malay counterparts differentiate things to be exchanged by their degrees of supernatural power. Here, I draw on Marcel Mauss's (1990) explication of the spirit embedded in things and people to describe the ways of exchange, group relations, and identity among the Orang Laut and the Malays. The Malays believe in the spirits embedded in things and people, and how all this is intricately tied in with, and can ultimately affect, their own being. Such a belief explains why they endeavour to protect themselves from things originating from an Orang Laut territory. For the Orang Laut and all their non-Orang Laut transactors, things are differentiated by the degree of supernatural power they possess. The following is a scaled discussion of these power-endowed things.

ADOPTED THINGS

The Orang Laut *piara* (adopt/care for) things that are of importance to them. The word *piara* is also used by both Orang Laut and Malays when they refer to the adoption of persons. Similarly to adopting a person, the Orang Laut explain that to adopt a thing entails taking care of, feeding, protecting, raising, maintaining, and guarding the thing. Things which can be adopted range from fishing equipment, *kebun*s (small plantations, gardens, or farm plots) to houses. To adopt these things also entails having to *jampi* them. This endows an adopted thing with supernatural powers. In the example given below, Meen, an Orang Laut from Teluk Nipah, explains why he must adopt his boat.

> Meen:
> I adopt my boat because I would not have enough to eat if I were to catch only Rp. 1,000 worth of fish each day. Therefore, in order to travel further away safely and to catch as much as, say, Rp. 40,000 worth of fish, I need to adopt my boat properly. I must feed and spellbind it to attain a good catch. To adopt my boat, or as the Chinese would say, to *kong* (bewitch) it, I have to feed it with *pulot* (glutinous rice) and *kachang* (nuts) by placing them in front and at the back of the boat.
>
> Yang (Meen's wife):
> This is to *jaga* (look after/protect) our boat so that outsiders will not disturb it.

Likewise, the following excerpts show how the Orang Laut adopt their houses and small gardens respectively.

> Halus:
> It is only when Ceco finishes building his kitchen that his whole house could be considered complete. Ceco will then adopt his house by casting a spell over it and offering a plate of glutinous rice, nuts, and an egg on each of the four corners of his house. These will have to be placed at the top and not at the bottom of the four corners of the house.
>
> Meen:
> If I were to adopt my small garden, I would have to give it *beras hitam* (black rice grains), *beras kuning* (yellow rice grains) and *beras merah* (red rice grains) to eat.[1] I would have to place these food offerings at the four corners and entrance of the garden. We must not clear away any of the wood and trees that surround the garden. By giving food to the garden, we are asking the garden to help and protect us. If I adopt my garden well, the garden will *pukul* (strike) any intruder who tries to enter it. In fact, if I adopt my garden very well, it will not even allow my wife to enter without me.

The Orang Laut adhere to the belief that in order to reap plentifully from one's possession, one has to adopt the thing well. More importantly, by adopting a thing, a bond is established between the owner and the thing. This is so because the owner, by deciding to adopt a thing, is also making a decision to merge the thing with his or her own identity which, in essence, is the soul. Therefore, to fail to adopt these things responsibly also means endangering one's well being. If the owner is negligent, the thing may be pummelled, harmed or become polluted by the invasion of a spirit that would either 'eat' the owner or cause danger to his or her well being.

Adopted things can also become polluted if prohibitions specific to them are not observed. One common example often cited by the Orang Laut is how their fishing nets become polluted.

> Meen:
> We adopt the things that we as fishing people would own. Therefore, if my *jaring* (a type of fishing net) is in front of my boat, your shoes must not step on it or I would not be able to catch any fish.[2] We also have to adopt our boat very well. If it *kena sampok* (becomes polluted), it would be very difficult for us to look for the correct medicine to cure it.

An adopted thing can therefore also be seen as a metonymic sign for the owner (Leach, 1989). If the sign is destroyed, the owner will also be damaged. Hence, one of the most feared dangers is letting adopted things fall prey to the evil intentions of outsiders. The outsiders would be able to harm and poison the owner through things which have a direct bearing on his well being.

However, this is not to say that adopted things cannot be alienated. For example, boats are often replaced with new ones. It is common for adopted things to be exchanged, given away, or sold. The bond between the owner and an adopted thing, and the meaning and power of an adopted thing, can be transformed by the way in which it is circulated through different regimes of value (Appadurai, 1995:4). Greater social value in a thing and a deeper bond with the owner are maintained in the adopted thing if it is circulated as a gift or a bartered object, rather than sold for money.

However, adopted things can only be given away or bartered between Orang Laut belonging to the same group. Reciprocity is involved in these two forms of exchange as a thing given away or bartered is often replaced with other things or services. Since adopted things are metonymic signs which embody the identity of the owner and can establish a spiritual bond between the transactors, it follows that they can only be given away or bartered between members of the same group. When a thing enters the sphere of inter-community transaction, selling for money becomes the preferred form of exchange. Money is a kind of safety valve to distance things from their owner, thereby reducing the dangers involved.

INALIENABLE (ADOPTED) POSSESSIONS

Hairpieces, musical instruments, *keris* (a wavy double-bladed dagger), sea shells, pounders, and pieces of rock are among the range of things that can become Orang Laut heirlooms. These are, in fact, most highly treasured things by the Orang Laut and the Malays alike as they are believed to contain inherent powers and an inalienable value. Unlike adopted things, their powers and value are not bestowed upon them through the adoptive efforts of their owner. Nor does any form of exchange for their circulation affect them. All effort is made to keep these things out of circulation, and even out of sight. Adapting Weiner's terminology (1985), I refer to these things as inalienable (adopted) possessions. I have bracketed the word 'adopted' to make the point that while the owners of such things usually make the effort to adopt them, these efforts merely enhance, but do not endow, the inherent magical powers and effectiveness of the things. On the other hand, the longer heirlooms are kept within a family or its descent groups, the more their value increases. Age adds value and so does the ability to keep a thing against all urgent needs and demands that might force a person or group to release it to others. Keeping them is therefore a creation of value (Weiner, 1985).

Suri, an Orang Laut from Pulau Nanga, possessed several highly treasured family heirlooms. Among them were *siput* (mollusca), a *lesung* (pounder) with a hole at its base, and a rock which the Pulau Nanga Orang Laut community maintained to be a gold nugget. Each of these items was believed to have immense supernatural powers, enhanced successively by spells pronounced upon them by many generations. For instance, water boiled with the pounder immersed in it and then poured through the hole of the pounder would be endowed with the supernatural powers of the pounder itself. Drinking such water would neutralize all poison in one's body that might have entered it while unwittingly eating or drinking anything poisoned by one's enemies. Drinking this water could also cure headaches and backaches. Bathing on Fridays with this water could also strengthen one's marriage by instilling faithfulness in one's spouse.

There was another pounder which Suri had inherited. Unlike the pounder with a hole at its bottom, this pounder was cracked into two pieces. The Orang Laut maintained that both pounders contained inherent supernatural powers, but that the one with the hole was the more powerful. Pounders with a hole at the bottom, compared with all other types of pounders, are believed to contain the most powerful sorts of supernatural qualities. For instance, the Orang Laut explained that one could immediately drink the water from the holed pounder as an antidote without spellbinding it further, but one might have to enhance the supernatural powers of the water from the cracked pounder in order to achieve the same effectiveness.

The seashells were also considered extraordinary. I was shown two: one with a naturally polished surface and the other with an extra cleft in its inner cover. They were said to possess magical powers to clear and sharpen one's vision. To activate their power, one only needs to rub the shells against one's eyelids. A cooling sensation would follow, and in the words of Suri, 'your eyes would sparkle.'

The rock, which was referred to as being 'given by God,' had been dislodged from the ground in a thunderstorm. It was believed to be so powerful in magical qualities that one did not even have to endow it with spells. According to the community, Suri had been extremely fortunate to notice and pick up this rock and adopt it, thus bringing to it its full measure of supernatural powers. Suri said that if she were to give this rock to someone else, the recipient, before going to sleep, could rub it against his or her eyelids, and he or she would be able to have a clear vision of where Suri was and what she was doing at that particular time, even if they were physically very far apart.

In the course of my fieldwork, a Malay woman from the neighbouring island of Karas came to Pulau Nanga in search of such Orang Laut heirlooms. She was willing to exchange from Rp. 10,000 to Rp. 50,000 for one of these heirlooms. The Malay woman first approached Bolong, the Headman of the Pulau Nanga community. He refused permission for these heirlooms to leave the community. He told the Malay woman that if she wished to pursue this matter further, she could personally approach his younger sister Suri, who had inherited these heirlooms. Meanwhile Bolong had secretly sent a message to Suri, informing her that a Malay woman was interested in these heirlooms, but on no account would he allow them to leave their community. Accordingly, Suri refused to enter into any negotiation with the Malay woman. This was Suri's explanation.

> Suri:
> These *buntat* (supernaturally endowed fortune telling things) are here to protect us. They are our *ilmu*. We do not want to give or sell them to anyone else. The Malay woman only wanted to possess them to harm others.

Inalienable (adopted) possessions such as family heirlooms participate in the soul of the owner and are thus metonymic signs. Unlike adopted things which can be transacted under certain circumstances, there is an indissoluble bond between family heirloom and its owner. Therefore, it would mean great danger if the Malay woman had gained possession of these things.

Weiner (1985:210-11), in her analysis of inalienable wealth, states that 'keeping these things instead of giving them away is essential to retaining one's social identity ... [and that] the primary value of inalienability, however, is expressed through the power these things have to define and locate who one is in a historical sense. The objects act as a vehicle for bringing past time into the present, so that the histories of ancestors, titles or mythological events become an intimate part of a person's present identity. To lose this claim to the past is to lose part of who one is in the present. The quality of sacredness increases the more these things are kept out of circulation.' An added significance of the Orang Laut's inalienable wealth is that it takes on important properties in affecting the symbolic boundaries in the hierarchy of what it means to be Malay.

After the episode with the Malay woman, Suri, who was my *mamak angkat* (adopted mother), discussed the issue with her husband and siblings. She decided with their agreement to give these heirlooms to me with the following explanation.

Suri:
Rather than having people like the Malay woman come to ask me to sell them these supernaturally endowed things, I will give them to people who have been very good to me. I have discussed this with my husband, Tekong, and my siblings. I have decided to give you these things ... The reason why I am giving them to you is because you have rendered sufficient help to me. When I die, you will be able to say that you are my descendant. These supernaturally endowed things will enable us never to be separated.

Cynthia:
But these things mean very much to you! How can I accept them?

Boat:
You cannot refuse what my elder sister is giving you. If someone from this community gives you something, you must accept.

In bequeathing these things to me in such a manner, Suri enabled me, an outsider, to claim descent from an Orang Laut if ever I should so desire. The Orang Laut community was drawing me symbolically into itself. I was reminded that by rubbing the stone against my eyelids, I could have a vision of my adopted mother and be one with her no matter what distance separated us. This was all due to the indissoluble bond that had been established by my adopted mother giving me these inalienable (adopted) heirlooms, and my receiving them. The supernatural power of the objects had already been enhanced by generations of Orang Laut who had possessed them. The life of the heirlooms was therefore now flowing into me and making me a descendant of this long chain of inheritors.

Thus, giving away these things also implies acknowledging the recipient as kin. If these things had been given to the Malay woman, an undesirable but indissoluble kinship tie would have been established with her. This tie would be undesirable for both the Orang Laut community and the Malay woman. From the perspective of the Orang Laut community, such an association would be dangerous. The Malays could and would easily contaminate their heirlooms for the purpose of poisoning them. For the Malays, any kinship tie with the Orang Laut is considered 'shameful' and undesirable. Such an association would link them with what is uncivilized, dirty, impure, and polluted. Therefore, the Malay woman attempted to sever this bond through the use of money in obtaining these things.

However, every effort is made to keep such things out of circulation and out of sight. Even when these things are given away, a list of conditions is imposed by the giver on the recipient. The following is an excerpt of Suri's stipulations when she handed me the heirlooms.

> Suri:
> Be sure that no one else gets what I have given you. The minute others see these things, they will want them, and will try to steal or take them away from you. You must promise never to give them to anyone else. If you do, others will lead a comfortable life, but not you. Instead, you will be the one who will lose out.

These conditions represent the range of solutions which enable one to keep while giving. When a thing is given away, the giver is not in any way divorced from his possession. Instead, the giver and the recipient become united as one through the thing. This is sealed with contracts and pledges from the recipient to the giver to continue to adopt the thing (Mauss, 1990). In so doing, the giver retains the status of owner in the object. Therefore, inalienable (adopted) things are the most feared, yet most desired, of all things by those outside the Orang Laut community. By offering money to the Orang Laut, the outsiders hope to obtain safely things they greatly desire.

Non-Adopted Things

These include anything owned and/or used but not adopted by the Orang Laut. In comparison with adopted and inalienable (adopted) things, non-adopted things can be distinguished as things of association. These things are seen as possessing less supernatural power. However, they are still associated with the Orang Laut. There are various reasons for this, e.g.,

1. Things which bear the craftsmanship of the Orang Laut. Examples include fishing spears, hand carved turtle-shell ornaments such as bangles, pendants, and hand-woven rattan baskets;
2. Things which embody the Orang Laut's practical activity and/or physical touch. Examples are speared maritime products, fruits, vegetables, and plants grown by them. This also includes all food, drinks, and cakes prepared by them; and
3. Things which have been passed over, been in contact or close association with the Orang Laut's body. Examples include their clothes and footwear.

The subsequent use by another person of things once associated with an Orang Laut could endanger both parties. These things are regarded as items which the Orang Laut can use to bewitch others. Otherwise, these things are relatively safe. According to my non-Orang Laut informants, these things may therefore be accepted as gifts by those whom my informants refer to as the 'braver people.' Below is an example of a difference in opinion between a Malay couple over the safety of such things. This concerned a Malay woman bringing home some coconuts which had been grown and given to her by an Orang Laut woman.

Ein, the son of the Malay couple, spotted the coconuts that his mother Pindah had in her kitchen. Immediately, he wanted to eat them.

Ahmad (the father):
Where did these coconuts come from?

Pindah:
Suri gave them to me.

Ahmad:
Suri? No one in this family is going to eat these coconuts. Throw them away immediately! You should have known better than to bring these coconuts home. We will be poisoned.

Pindah:
I thought these coconuts would be all right [safe] since they were not opened.

Ahmad:
Opened or unopened coconuts, we are not going to kill ourselves. Your greed for just a few coconuts will kill us. They [Orang Laut] can even poison these unopened coconuts.

The difference in opinion between this Malay couple also reflects the differing opinions of the other non-Orang Laut groups regarding things that may or may not be accepted as gifts from the Orang Laut.[3] In the course of my field trips, the only things that were ever accepted by the 'braver' non-Orang Laut as gifts were the non-adopted things. Nevertheless, should the recipient subsequently suffer any adversity, it would be blamed upon the recipient's association with the thing which had come from the Orang Laut.

Yet why would the Orang Laut even oblige these Malays? The Orang Laut would usually offer me the explanation that in tracing their genealogy, the Malays could be seen as related to them through inter-group marriage with one of their ancestors. However, just as interestingly, as soon as the Malays were out of Orang Laut territory, they would vehemently protest against the Orang Laut's earlier claim of kinship ties. Below is an excerpt from a Malay woman's protest.

Pindah:
What an insult! How could she [Orang Laut] say that we are like sisters, or that we look alike? I am Malay and she is Orang Laut. Anyone can see the difference. Of course I did not dare disagree in her presence in case she felt insulted and would poison me. In my heart, I was telling myself, 'She is insane!' Of course we are not the least bit related. My mother and father must not hear of this or they would be deeply insulted.

From Pindah's protest, it is clear that this kinship relation is often disputed. The Orang Laut are aware of this disclaimer and all the more mistrust the Malays who refute their kinship ties. Therefore, with few exceptions, the Orang Laut only give non-adopted things to the Malays, things which pose less danger to both groups. These things can also be sold. This is, in fact, the preferred form of inter-group exchange for the circulation of things.

When something is given by the Orang Laut to an outsider, it is usually treated with suspicion and disposed of almost immediately when the recipient is out of sight of the Orang Laut. Likewise, the Orang Laut fear and dispose of all things received as gifts from either another group of Orang Laut or a non-Orang Laut source. Exceptions to this rule are gifts from the Chinese (see Chapter 7). These are accepted without fear or suspicion.

METONYMIC SIGNS

Things are metonymic signs for their owners. In Chapter 1, I outlined the logic by which signs and symbols are connected so that things become the metonymic signs for their owners and how these metaphoric condensations explain the system of social classification for the Orang Laut in the Malay World. This social classification erects symbolic boundaries between the Orang Laut and the Malays; these boundaries, in turn, dictate the forms of exchange that they can or cannot engage in with each other and the types of things that they can circulate. The significance of this all is that it ultimately defines the identity of the peoples in the Malay World.

Material artefacts and skills, as well as the appropriation or avoidance of these things, forges a multitude of issues that have many ramifications for how societies perceive of themselves, and for how we understand societies. Exchange is always a process negotiation which reflects either personal and/or wider social relationships. The dynamics of the social situation emerge at the moment of a transaction to reflect who one's affines, strangers, enemies or friends are, as well as the morality or immorality of giving or taking from one exchange partner or another (Thomas, 1991:8).

NOTES

1 These uncooked rice grains were dyed by several methods. Sometimes artificial food colouring was used. However, more often than not, the Orang Laut would pound natural ingredients for the needed dye. As an example, pounded *kunyit* (yellow ginger or turmeric) is usually chosen to provide a yellow dye when needed.
2 Endicott (1991:116) suggests that 'the prohibition on wearing shoes or *sarong*s and on carrying umbrellas in mines and fishing stakes may exist because these too strongly recall civilisation to be ignored by the spirits.' While Smedal (1989:88) in his study on the *Orang Lom* agrees that this may be true in the peninsula context, he thinks that a similar interpretation in the Lom case would miss the point. He argues that in the Lom case, the prohibitions are less in order to appease the *semangat* (soul) than to preserve cultural difference.

3   The Malays have varying opinions concerning the degree of danger between unopened and opened fruits, food and drinks from untorn packaging, raw as opposed to cooked food, cold as compared to hot food and drinks, and food and drinks out of a common pot in contrast to individual portions.

Chapter 6

Sharing and Helping: Constructions of the Orang Laut's Identity

Picture 6: Pui's *kenduri besar*, the big religious feast

This chapter looks at how and what it means for the Orang Laut to circulate things within their own communities. It examines how the meanings of objects are defined or transformed through different forms of exchange. It also details the social relations and group solidarity that are established through the circulation of things.

Within their communities, the Orang Laut observe the principle of sharing and helping as an extension of their system of reciprocity. Their network of sharing and helping operates in the same social context as their system of gift exchange. The individuals within a community who give things to one another are also the people who help and share things at a household or community level. There are, however, differences in social relations. Reciprocity in gift giving constitutes a relationship between two parties (Sahlins, 1974:188), while sharing and helping represents a collective group action.

The conventional anthropological approach to analysing exchange networks has been linked with reciprocity (see, for example, Mauss, 1990; Polanyi, 1944; Sahlins, 1974; Lomnitz, 1977). The perspective I adopt in this chapter parallels that of Sneath (1993:196) in that I am 'not suggesting that reciprocity is unnecessary in the analysis, simply that it is not the defining characteristic of the relationships that form networks.' Reciprocity is based upon relationships of social obligation. For this reason, I believe that it is the obligation rather than the exchange aspect of the relationship that is more useful in understanding the significance of the Orang Laut's networks of sharing and helping.

Many obligations between the Orang Laut are enacted along the connective and cementing networks of sharing and helping and barter exchange. Reasons for why and how the Orang Laut choose to circulate things within their community in such ways can be understood on two levels. On the one hand, sharing, helping, and non-profit-making barter exchanges are representations of ideal behaviour for the Orang Laut. They imply egalitarian status, if not generosity between the transactors. As an example, the movement of food, in particular maritime products, expresses group solidarity. In this instance, money can even enter the picture. In the transaction, money is converted into a 'thing' that will do something else, such as purchase food or white burial cloth, for other Orang Laut in need. These forms of exchange endow values for the things being exchanged and seek to establish a deeper bond between the transactors. On the other hand, intra-community sharing, helping, and barter exchanges also carry a symbolic load of insider and outsider relations. They aim at restricting the circulation of things to insiders only. These forms of exchange construct and maintain group boundaries for the Orang Laut and Malays. They perpetuate demarcations of *orang kita* (us/insiders) from *orang lain* (them/outsiders) and determine who may or may not be the participants of a transaction.

In reality there may be little or no actual sense of solidarity among the Orang Laut themselves. Yet the Orang Laut feel that they ought to have or at least to display a sense of group unity through their network of exchanges. Since one important motivating factor in fulfilling their obligations of sharing and helping is self-interest on the part of calculating individuals, the ambiguities in the Orang Laut's network of giving, sharing and helping, barter exchange, and selling are intentional and significant. They serve to combine and/or reinforce the principles governing all forms of exchange. Such ambiguities are intended to allow things to circulate within the community without unduly curtailing calculated self-interest. They facilitate the exchange of things and services without weakening group solidarity.

The Orang Laut use the words '*kasih*' ('give') and/or '*tukar*' ('exchange') to describe the ways in which they circulate things within their communities. The word '*jual*' (sell) is seldom used here, even when money is involved. That is to say, the word 'sell' is used only when things are circulated between an Orang Laut community and a non-Orang Laut community. It is quite common to hear the Orang Laut complain of not receiving gifts from other members of their community. This is because the idea of a pure or free gift (Malinowski, 1922) does not exist with them to begin with. When an Orang Laut gives something to another member of the community, the thing given is never referred to as a *kado* (gift/present). At the very most, it would be said to render *bantu* (help). Frequent networks of sharing and helping take place among the Orang Laut within the same group, and they range from exchanges between individuals to exchanges between households at the community level.

SHARING AND HELPING BETWEEN INDIVIDUALS WITHIN ORANG LAUT COMMUNITIES

Exchanges of food, fishing equipment, houses, and labour occur almost on a daily basis between individuals within an Orang Laut group. Such exchanges are preceded by house visits which may at times include a trip to the home of kin on another island. Both formal and informal visits are ways of publicly declaring the harmony of social relations. When social relations break, all communication ties, visits, and other forms of exchange cease at the same time.

The Orang Laut often give each other raw and cooked food. The sharing of maritime products is of particular significance. It is one product which has so far withstood monetization in intra-community exchanges. In this respect, it stands in sharp contrast to all other objects of exchange. Maritime products varying from fish and crustaceans to mollusca and edible sea cucumbers constitute the paramount sign of identity for the Orang Laut. To be an Orang Laut is synonymous with being a skilled fishing person who can survive by the harvest from the sea. Although rice and, to a lesser extent, sago seem to be gaining in popularity today, it is still maritime products which constitute the staple.

As remarked by Sahlins (1974:215), 'staple foodstuffs cannot always be handled just like anything else. Socially, they are not like anything else.' The Orang Laut do not sell or barter their maritime products within their community. It is one category of things above all others which, when shared, connotes solidarity and goodwill.

Lacet's family had just returned from a fishing trip. Yearning for fish cooked with pineapple, he heard that his sister Suri had just prepared some. He brought pieces of his raw fish to give her and asked for some of her cooked food. Suri accepted his raw fish and reciprocated with rice and some fish cooked with pineapple. This is an example of an immediate reciprocation of raw food for cooked food. When Lacet brought his raw fish to Suri, he said that he was 'giving' it to her. This act of 'giving' would often be spoken of as 'helping' at a later date. Yet, at the same time, he expected her to respond to his request for fish cooked with pineapple and she accordingly obliged.

However, in most cases, the 'giving' is not reciprocated immediately. For instance, the Orang Laut consider turtle meat a delicacy. Occasionally, an Orang Laut is able to catch a turtle. When this happens, there is much excitement within the community. This is partly because members of the community are aware that the turtle caught will usually be of such a size that it could be cut into portions to be shared among all. The person who caught the turtle would then give the other members in the community a piece of the meat. In one such instance, Pui's family had caught a huge turtle. News of her family's catch spread around Pulau Nanga immediately. After Pui had cut a sizeable portion of the turtle for her own family's consumption, the rest was soon given to other members of the community. Pui herself gave these either to people of her choice or to those in the community who had come to ask for a portion. As long as there was still enough turtle to be shared, none of those who had come and asked Pui for a portion were refused. Pui was obliged to share and not to turn down anyone.

The distinction between 'shares' and 'sharing' is crucial (Bodenhorn, 1989:83). The division of certain catches, such as a huge turtle, into 'shares' is expected; the members of the community to whom one must distribute the shares are in principle not pre-determined. Pui could decide with whom she would share the meat as long as she also did so with those who personally approached her with a request. She was also under great pressure to share it with her extended family. In this network of sharing and helping, 'food is something over which relatives have rights, and conversely relatives are people who provide or take toll on one's food' (Richards, 1939:200).[1] The amount of turtle meat that Pui kept for herself was significantly larger than the amount that any other single household would receive through sharing.

Embedded in the act of sharing and helping are the knowledge and an unwritten contract between giver and recipient that whatever is given must be reciprocated at some point of time in the future. The delay in reciprocity establishes a bond of trust between the transactors and aims at waiting without forgetting. The very act of Pui distributing her turtle meat to the public -- that is, beyond her extended family -- indicates two things. First, her reciprocity to those from whom she had previously received shares of meat. Second, investing by way of the fruits of her labour for the future.

The Orang Laut's system of sharing resources profits the individual in the community. In the case of Pui's surplus turtle meat, this sharing system spreads out small portions of food for her and the rest of the community. As meat easily rots in a hot climate, it is actually disadvantageous for an individual to hoard a large amount. Since in time, a participating person receives back in small portions about the same amount of food he contributes in a large amount at the point of giving, no food is wasted in this system. The people are able to consume more meat than they could have done if they did not share. The total amount of food available to the group within this system of sharing is thus greater than the amount that would be available to all the individual members had they tried to consume it individually. Everyone profits by this system. The result is that the individual will willingly contribute food, or for that matter, any other resources. This is not just because it is thought right to do so but because it is to one's advantage. The sharing of resources involves economic ties that make the Orang Laut group more stable than they might otherwise be. Furthermore, a person can rely on the other members of their community sharing their resources with them because their sharing ultimately benefits themselves (Dentan, 1979:50).

Yet this does not mean that the Orang Laut do not exercise calculation in order to avoid sharing their surplus. These attempts are covered up to prevent accusations of *lokek* (selfishness, stinginess, miserliness), and the schemers themselves being edged out of the community's network from which they stand to profit. Wee (1985:83) suggests that the Orang Laut are not interested in fishing methods that would bring in a greater quantity of fish than is needed for their daily needs. They are not even keen on salting their fish for preservation. She maintains that the Orang Laut find such methods 'not suitable' and 'counter-productive for an economy based on day-to-day subsistence.' While there is some plausibility in Wee's statement, I examine another reason offered by my Orang Laut informants in view of their network of sharing and helping. Lampong and his wife Siti secretly explained why they, like the other members of their community, chose not to salt their extra fish for future consumption.

> Lampong:
> We know that we can salt fish and keep them for difficult days. However, if we were to do that, many people would not go out to sea to work. They would just ask us for dried fish. If all of us go out to sea to work together, we will be able to have fish to eat. [Under such circumstances,] should my siblings not catch anything, and ask me for fish, I would give. Likewise, should I not have anything, and ask my siblings for help, they too would give me something. [This would be fair.] If we all worked together, we would all be able to have fresh fish to eat immediately. If some were not to work, then they would constantly be coming to ask for extra fish. We still do salt and dry some fish for days when we are too lazy to go out to sea. However, it is something that we do not want to do very much.

> Siti:
> Yes, as soon as the fish is dried at about three in the afternoon, people come and ask for the fish. What can we do? We cannot say, 'No!' People would say that we are selfish. We have to give. The fish disappear as soon as they are dried! What is the point of us salting our fish?

> Lampong:
> We might as well sell all our fish or cook everything at once and eat them all ourselves.

The issue here is therefore not a matter of mere unsuitability to 'an economy based on day-to-day subsistence' as proposed by Wee (1985:83), but of not wanting to share.

Food dealings are 'a delicate barometer, a ritual statement as it were, of social relations' (Sahlins, 1974:215). Food is thus used as 'a starting, a sustaining, or a destroying mechanism of sociability' (*ibid*). On the one hand, the Orang Laut feel obliged to share food even if they do not want to. On the other hand, they continue to share food for fear of seeming to calculate gains and losses. Underlying all this is a fear that should they offend another in their pool of potential partners in the system of sharing and helping, it could jeopardize their chances of receiving necessary resources from others at a future time of need. Extra care is taken not to be stingy with people who possess high-demand specialized resources. Lampung explains that one such person in the community is the midwife.

> Lampong:
> My elder sister Suri possesses the skill for delivering babies. Therefore, it would be wise not to be selfish with her.

The obligation to share and help is a calculated expectation of delayed reciprocity from the recipient. Lampung's statements can be read as: the failure to give and reciprocate would establish a norm of selfishness.

The Orang Laut employ social sanctions to exert pressure on members of the community to share their food. The Orang Laut have (I assume) borrowed the term '*dosa*' (sin) from mainstream religions around them to describe the danger of not sharing one's surplus food, especially when asked to, with other members of the community, in particular the elderly, the sick, the dying, and pregnant women. Yang Ama, a young pregnant woman, did not have any food in her house. She approached her father's younger sister Suri for raw fish. Suri obliged without hesitation. This was Suri's explanation.

> Suri:
> If Yang Ama had asked me for anything else, I could have refused to give it. However, Yang Ama is pregnant and she desires to eat fish. I cannot refuse her. It is because if she develops complications during childbirth and dies, I will have sinned against her forever. You must never refuse a pregnant woman food when she asks for it. Yang Ama is like a daughter to me. She is my eldest brother Bolong's daughter.

The Orang Laut do not expect to be reciprocated immediately, although there is an unspoken understanding that the recipients and their family must reciprocate to the giver or the giver's family in their future times of need. Residing in the same area of kinspeople is to some extent a function of the sharing of food and help. The exchange of food, as contended by Gow (1991), also constitutes a central part of the idiom of ties between real kin. However, for the Orang Laut and Malays, the sharing of and helping one another with food also implies that people, whether or not they are genetically related, can become related through this act of food sharing (Carsten, 1991; McKinley, 1981).

SHARING AND HELPING:
THE RELATION BETWEEN HOUSEHOLD AND COMMUNITY

In the event of a serious illness or death of a member of the community, visits by one's kin, especially from those within the community, become regular and expected. In such circumstances, the entire community's participation, as compared to ad hoc individual household participation, is expected. The focus is on the in-gathering of the whole community with representatives from as many households of the entire community as possible. Members of the community are expected to share and help one another with food, labour, money, and whatever extra resources they may have for alleviating the difficulties of the family concerned. There are, however, no specific rules pertaining to the amount of anything that has to be shared. Below are two examples of how this system of sharing and helping operated during the illnesses of Ross and Endi and the subsequent death of the latter. They were both members of the Pulau Nanga Orang Laut community.

Ross contracted a venereal disease from her husband Lacet.[2] Her condition deteriorated rapidly as the days passed into weeks. Throughout the long period of Ross's illness, Lacet was unable to carry out his daily fishing activities. As soon as Lacet informed the community, comprised mainly of his siblings, of his plight, everyone was obliged to pay regular visits to his family. This is how Lacet described their visits.

Lacet:
Siti-payong came to give me fish. Den also gave us turtle meat.[3] At five last evening, Den came to cast a spell over Ross.[4] I was angry with him for not helping to cast a spell over her earlier. I told him, 'You have the *ilmu*, why don't you help?' Too many people have been trying to cast spell over Ross so it has not been effective. *Gabung, lawan lawan dia punya jampi itu* [These different spells counteract each other]. She is much better now. Den is too shy to cast spells if there are too many people around. It is because he knows there are others who are powerful in their *ilmu*. But Den has great in-depth *ilmu*. He is one of the best around.

A while ago, we thought of taking Ross to the doctor. She was feeling dizzy and we were afraid she would fall out of the *pom-pom* (a motorized boat) and drown. Ceco came to cast a spell over her so that she would not die.[5] He has the *ilmu* for this particular need. The white [crosses] that he drew on her feet and hands and at our doorstep were to protect her. He had cast a spell over the *kapur* (slaked lime) to draw [the crosses] on her.

Suri's eldest daughter Yang came to cook for us last night. Suri's family has been helping us most because her family and mine are *biak* (on good terms). Whenever I have extra money, I give her some. Therefore, when I am ill, she comes to help me. When I have extra fish, I give them to Suri too. We eat the fish together. Yang is also washing our clothes. A few days ago, Suri gave us rice with soy sauce.

Most of my siblings would help, but there are some who would not. Kassim's wife Ani has not helped at all. When Ani was ill, we helped her. When her father died, we helped her too. I am now very angry with her. Ani and my wife Ross share the same father, but each has a different mother. Ani is therefore my sister-in-law. Even before Ani's father died, we always helped her, but she has never bothered to help us.

Itam, who is also Ross's sister, came over once. She gave us Rp. 1,000 to buy milk for our children, because Ross was ill and unable to breast feed our children. Itam said she would not be able to come over any more because she is too busy with her children. She does not have her own boat to row over when her husband takes their only boat out. It is difficult for her to row over with her babies without any help.

Right now, whoever pities us will come and give us fish. We will accept. There are some who give, and some who do not. If there are people who know that I do not have any rice, they will come and help. People will also help me throw out the water from my boat if I ask for help. If my in-laws were here, they would help me too.

But it does not matter because if it is I who need their help today, it may be their turn to ask me for help tomorrow. If they are sick, I shall help them too, but not Ani. When Ani delivered her two children, Ross went to help her. Now that Ross is ill, she has not come to help us at all! Ani has made no effort to come over for even a day to help cook for us. If she helped a bit, I would not be so angry. When Ross recovers, I shall not allow her to help Ani again.

Lacet's description of his siblings' visits during his wife's illness can be compared to that of the visits which Endi, a baby boy in the community, received during his period of grave illness. He was Den's son.

Endi had been ill for four days. This disrupted his family's fishing activities. When his father, Den, told the community of his family's situation, the community, comprised mainly of Den's siblings, started visiting him. Den's siblings came and gave him money. They explained this was to help Den's family purchase basic necessities such as 'an injection for

Endi, and rice, sugar, and cigarettes for the family.' Den's siblings also hurried over to cast spells over a delirious Endi. Ceco, Den's older brother, was the first to rush over. He cast a spell over a bottle of ointment before rubbing it onto Endi. This visit was closely followed by Den's other siblings. They too helped cast spells over the baby. Boat, Den's younger brother, explained that Endi's illness was 'difficult and complicated.'[6]

After a close examination of the structure of Den's house, Ceco advised Den to move Endi out of the place. Ceco directed Den's attention to the latter's incorrect house construction that had permitted the entry of evil spirits. Upon hearing Ceco's instructions, Boat quickly offered Den's family refuge in his house. The family moved into Boat's house. Den's siblings continued to visit his family in Boat's house. Like his siblings, Den attempted to cast a spell over his son. However, Boat stopped him. Boat told Den that he could see from experience that the baby's eyes showed that 'father and son did not *cocok* (match harmoniously).' Instead, Boat told Den to leave the casting of spells to others in the community.

Expectations and obligations to share and help become more marked during periods of a community member's sickness or death. Everyone in the community with surplus food or money is expected to share and help. Only members of a community or kin from related communities are involved in this system of sharing and helping. If close kin or a co-villager does not pay a visit and offer something to help the family in need, their behaviour is described as selfish and bad mannered. At times of need, non-participation in exchanges between kin members puts the bond at risk.

Things from non-Orang Laut, especially the Malays, are viewed with suspicion and as a rule rejected. Yet it is sometimes necessary for the Orang Laut families undergoing a crisis to obtain things like rice, sugar, and even the white cloth for burial purposes from those whom they perceive to be 'outsiders.' The giving of money by their community hence reflects the awareness that money is needed to purchase these things from the outside.

Responsibility for taking care of the sick is in many cases almost completely taken out of the hands of the immediate family and made a matter of general concern for the entire community. Den, for example, was advised by Boat not to interfere with the casting of spells over his son.

Endi died in Boat's house the very evening that his family moved into the latter's home. Endi's body was not brought back to his own home. Instead, his corpse was prepared for burial in Boat's house. Preparation for Endi's burial was very much in the hands of the members of the community. The community contributed money to Den for the purchase of a piece of white cloth to wrap Endi's body for burial. I was also approached for a contribution towards the buying of cakes and beverages for the first *kenduri* to be held immediately after the burial. If I had not obliged, Den would have had to use the money given to him by his community to buy the necessary things for the *kenduri*.

The obligations to give, receive, and reciprocate in the system of helping and sharing are also a demonstration of unity in the community, as expressed in the communal ritual, the *kenduri*. It is held to mark deaths, marriages, the appeasing of spirits, and adoptions (of both things and children). A *kenduri* can vary greatly in scale or size, showing a continuum stretching from the home to the community (Carsten, 1987:165). It may include members of the immediate nuclear family only, or all members of the entire community. It delineates a social boundary within which people are cooperatively related, and the division between insiders and outsiders becomes most marked at the *kenduri*. The basic activity at these religious feasts is that food is eaten together by all at the same time.

The significance of exchanges of food between households lies in the obligation to give, receive, and reciprocate which holds the community together. The continuity of the household in the community is expressed in the symbolism of food sharing. In a *kenduri*, a symbolic 'phantasmagoric house' is created whereby adult members of the community gather together 'to consume food of a superior quality to that consumed in mere material houses' (Carsten, 1987:166). The community represents itself as a household via the *kenduri*. It is 'stronger and more powerful than the individual household ... The household yields to the community which controls its function of food sharing' (Carsten, 1987:165).

As Endi's parents sat aside grieving over the death of their son, other members of the community came in to wash, powder, and perfume Endi's corpse. In the meantime the men from the community, including Lacet, were outside digging a grave. When the grave was almost ready, a message was sent to Boat's house, whereupon those who were professed Christians knelt by the corpse to say a prayer for the baby. The members of the community explained that it would have been preferable to have a Christian pastor carry out the last rites. Unfortunately, there was no such person within close proximity.

Den's siblings were aware that although Den was a professed Christian, he had never 'prayed' in 'the Christian way' before. Neither was he familiar with the rituals needed for a Christian burial. Tekong, another professed Christian and the only literate member of the community, was therefore asked to pray for Endi's soul. Tekong consulted his community about the matter. Subsequently, I was asked if I could do them the favour of praying and reading something from the Bible. It did not matter if they could not understand the English-language Bible that I had with me at that time. All that mattered was that I was to 'recite something powerful' for the soul. Once this was over, Den with his wife beside him carried the corpse to its grave. The community formed a procession behind Den and his wife. They carried an umbrella over Endi's body and threw yellow rice at Den's family to ward off evil spirits. The other members of the community did the burying of the corpse.

After the burial, Den hosted a *kenduri* for the community. The things that I had bought for the *kenduri* were passed on to Den's sister Suri, who was to oversee the arrangements for the *kenduri*. Neither Den nor his wife was in any way actively involved in the preparations; community participation was stressed throughout the affair. However, matters did not proceed without incident. Suri took advantage of her position in 'helping' with the preparations to siphon off half of the cakes and beverages that I had given to Den's family. While everyone was busy with the other arrangements concerning Endi's death, Suri enlisted her daughter's help in smuggling the cakes and beverages to their own home. The other members of the community were clearly aware of and unhappy about Suri's undertakings. However, there was no open confrontation with Suri as it was a time to stress community harmony and maintain peace. Much gossip followed afterwards.

A *kenduri* for the dead is held daily during the first forty days after the person's death. Thereafter, it is held once every ten days until the hundredth day.[7] These are usually minor occasions where either only the immediate family is involved or food is simply offered to the deceased. A climax is reached with a *kenduri besar* (big religious feast) on the one hundredth day after the death of the person. The entire community is invited to participate in the *kenduri besar*. Thereafter there is no need to hold another *kenduri* for the deceased until or unless someone dreams of the deceased asking to be fed.

Pui's family in Pulau Nanga hosted a *kenduri besar* to mark the hundredth day after the death of her mother, Isah. This *kenduri* was concurrently held to adopt me as a member of the community. There was much excitement in the community as the time approached, largely because Pui had made known that her husband Jiba was going to trap and slaughter a *pelanduk* (mouse-deer) for the feast. The community considered this meat a delicacy. The excitement in the community centred very much on the fact that they were 'going to eat mouse-deer' rather than to observe the hundredth day after the death of Isah.

As Pui issued invitations to the *kenduri*, she also approached the women for help with the preparation of food and cakes for the occasion. As noted by McKinley (1981:369), among the Malays it is also the case that 'the sharing of work in preparation for many household and neighbourhood feasts is one of the experiences which causes good friends to become "like siblings".' On the day of the *kenduri besar*, members of the community came to help Pui prepare a variety of food and cakes. This included boiled rice, curried mouse-deer with potatoes, boiled eggs, *wajik* (a cake made of glutinous rice and palm sugar), *kue rokok* (pastry rolled up to look like cigars, hence its name '*rokok*' or cigarettes), *kue ku*[8] (rice cake filled with crushed mung beans), and *kue baluh* (small cakes made from flour, eggs, and margarine). Tea and cigarettes were served to accompany the food and cakes. Pui herself was also directly involved in the preparation of these things.

The *kenduri besar* was not held until after four in the afternoon to coincide with the time of Isah's death. During the *kenduri besar*, Bolong, the Headman of the Pulau Nanga Orang Laut community, was called upon to offer the feast to Isah. Adult men and women sat together to form a ring around the food. I was asked to sit and eat with them. Throughout the *kenduri*, the guests from the community continually gave me food and cakes. The children were not allowed to join in the feasting until the adults had finished eating.

The *kenduri* of the Orang Laut as described above bears some similarity to the *kenduri* of the Malays. Both are known for the richness of the food served. There is considerable uniformity in the food served in all *kenduri*s of an Orang Laut community. The intention is not to rival one's neighbours by hosting a different feast. Instead, the focus is on offering a similar display to those of the others. A *kenduri* is neither an 'individual occasion that is being celebrated' nor an opportunity to accommodate 'individual expression.' Rather, it is a 'communal event' that is 'expressed in the notion of the surrender of the house' to the community (Carsten, 1987:164-5).

During the minor *kenduri*s, it was usually Isah's husband Awang Bai who offered the deceased the food that was laid out at the feast. However, at this *kenduri besar* which was to be a feast to symbolize the community in unity, the Headman was called upon to perform this function. Everyone present at the *kenduri* eats very quickly. Once the people have finished eating, they all help to clean up. For the Orang Laut, any food left over from a *kenduri* is distributed to the community. The focus here, as with the *kenduri*s hosted by the Malays, is on the 'cooperative effort' of the community (Carsten, 1987:163).

Significantly, one of the ways[9] chosen by the Orang Laut to adopt me as a member of their community was via my sharing and eating their food at a *kenduri*.[10] Previous to the *kenduri*, I had already been eating with them in different homes. The *kenduri* further cemented my relationship of belonging-ness with them. Thereafter, when introducing me to their kin from other communities, the Orang Laut of Pulau Nanga would always take great pride in stressing the fact that I had 'eaten' with them. The fact that I had without fear and inhibitions eaten with them was synonymous to my being regarded thereafter as an insider and no longer an outsider.

In contrast to a Malay *kenduri* where as many as possible of the members of the community are made to participate in the preparatory work, community participation at this stage on the part of the Orang Laut is on a much smaller scale. Also, unlike the *kenduri* of the Malays where '[it] is taken out of the hands of the individuals who are hosting it to be taken over by the community' (Carsten, 1987:162-3), it is not uncommon to find an Orang Laut host also actively engaged in the preparation. This can be seen from the case of Jiba hunting for the mouse-deer and Pui making the cakes for their *kenduri besar*. For the Malays, behaviour at the *kenduri* becomes very formal once the feasting gets under way. Men and women occupy different areas. In comparison, an Orang Laut *kenduri* can be either formal or be conducted in a very much more relaxed atmosphere where jokes may be told and alcohol consumed freely.[11] It is also not uncommon for men and women to sit together.

However, the place of children in both Orang Laut and Malay *kenduri*s is similar. The children had to sit behind the adults at Pui's *kenduri*. They ate only after the adults had finished eating. The rule is that the *kenduri* is for the adults and not for the children of the community. If the children eat before the adults, then the *kenduri* is considered wasted. The host is seen as having *rugi* (made a loss) and regarded as not having hosted the *kenduri* at all. Below is an example of such an instance at the first *kenduri* held immediately after Endi's burial.

Den:
What you gave for the *kenduri* was sufficient. However, we have lost because it was the children but not the adults who helped us, who ate all the biscuits and drank the Milo. This is not the right way for things to be done. Except for Boat who managed to drink a glass of Milo, none of my other siblings were able to get anything. You did not even get a glass of Milo. Yang [Den's wife] and myself were too angry to have anything. I tried to ask the children to go away, but they stayed to help themselves. I could not scold the children, as they are not mine. I am now *malu* (ashamed) that my siblings were not given anything for all that they had given us during our time of difficulty. … Lacet had given us rice when we could not go fishing because of Endi's illness.

Mazuk:
You did not do anything wrong. You gave sufficiently. We noticed what you gave. However, Den and you have lost because the adults did not get to eat anything. The *kenduri* is meant for adults, especially for those who have helped. It is not for the children.

Den:
I am angry at my *adik* (younger sibling) [Suri] for keeping the tin of Milo for herself. The tin of Milo that you gave was for the *kenduri*. The wrong person was put in charge of the *kenduri*.

Children who represent the closest of consanguineal kinship bonds (Carsten, 1987:162) tend to be disruptive of the basic function of a *kenduri*, which is visibly to forge the unity of the community rather than to reinforce close individual bonds of kinship in any given household. They are not accorded full membership in the community, as they are not yet able to enter into any decision-making process with regard to concerns of the wider community. Notwithstanding, it is interesting to see how an invitation to a *kenduri* – one of a very few – from the neighbouring island of Sembur was received by the Orang Laut of Pulau Nanga. Mainly Malays populated Pulau Sembur, and the invitation came from the Headman acting on behalf of the island's mosque to those among the Orang Laut of Pulau Nanga who had converted to Islam. The *kenduri* to which the Orang Laut had been invited was to celebrate the start of *Hari Raya Puasa*, or the end of the fasting month for the Muslims. All guests including the Orang Laut were asked to bring some food or cakes to contribute towards the *kenduri*.

On the appointed day, the Orang Laut did not bother to turn up for the *kenduri*. Instead, they carried on with their regular fishing activities. When I asked Bolong, the Headman of the Orang Laut, if he intended to attend the *kenduri*, he told me that he had better things to do, such as catching fish. In the meantime, the Malays in Pulau Sembur were kept waiting. Finally, the *kenduri* was held without the presence of any Orang Laut representative. Later, when the Orang Laut were asked about their absence, they replied nonchalantly, 'We did not have any eggs to make cakes for the *kenduri*, so we did not go.' This caused much anger and dismay among the Malays of Pulau Sembur. They began to criticize the Orang Laut behind their backs: 'What? No eggs! They are simply giving a poor excuse. It is unbelievable. It is only once a year that we hold such a *kenduri*. They call themselves *Orang Islam* (Muslims), but they do not even step into the mosque to pray ... Now they do not even bother to come just this once for the *kenduri*. This is what we mean. They are not Muslims, they are *orang lain* (outsiders).'

Very few – if any – invitations are issued by the Malays to the Orang Laut. If any invitation is issued, it is always connected with the obligation to observe some event involving the Islamic religion rather than commemorating, say, a marriage or death. The Orang Laut do not deem it necessary to attend these *kenduri*s hosted by the Malays. This stems from the fact that they do not desire to express visibly any solidarity with the Malays in spite of their having adopted the Islamic religion. In comparison, intra-Orang Laut community invitations to *kenduri*s are mostly accepted by other Orang Laut members of the community. It is important for the Orang Laut to reciprocate attendance at another Orang Laut's *kenduri*. However, signs of change are emerging within Orang Laut communities. Those who have felt obliged to adopt Islam are no longer allowed to eat pork.[12] These members have therefore to decide whether or not to attend the *kenduri* of a non-Muslim member of the community.

BEYOND SHARING AND HELPING: MONEY AND BARTER

The consequences of the introduction of money into the Orang Laut economy have been vast. It has brought the forbidden element of calculation into blossom. The Orang Laut have realized that money, unlike food, does not spoil, so that sharing is unnecessary to increase their individual wealth. Also, they have found it easier to hide money, leading to the dual benefit of finding it easier to avoid their obligation to share on the one hand, and making it more difficult to be identified as 'selfish' on the other. However, once money is used to buy extra food from the outside, they are under pressure to share again. If an Orang Laut buys ingredients to make cakes and decides to circulate the surplus within the community, they are expected to share rather than to sell them. Asmah and her daughter occasionally made cakes to sell to other members of their Pulau Nanga community. Although others bought Asmah's cakes, she was constantly criticized for selling rather than sharing her cakes.

> Pui:
> Asmah is the only person in this community who sells us the cakes that she makes. No one else does it.
>
> Suri:
> She is not ashamed.
>
> Pui:
> I would not sell cakes here. If I make extra cakes, I give them away. After all, everyone here is family. Unlike Asmah, I will never be able to take or ask my relatives for their money.
>
>
> Baggong:

She even asks us to pay her the money owed to her only two days ago. She is Malay. She is not an Orang Laut.

Suri:
Wait and see how it is when I make extra cakes. I shall give an equal share to all my siblings here. I shall never sell them my cakes.

Asmah's late mother was the second wife of Apong, father of Suri and Ceco. Asmah's mother was Malay. Her first husband was also Malay. They had three children, of whom Asmah was one. According to my Malay informants, Asmah's mother had been bewitched into marrying Apong. When Asmah's mother *ikut* Apong to live in the Orang Laut community, she took Asmah with her. Asmah later married her stepbrother, Ceco. In spite of the fact that Asmah had grown up and lived in an Orang Laut community for most of her life, her Malayness and 'outsider' status were constantly mentioned because of her breach in their network of sharing and helping.

Engaging in intra-community business activities places the Orang Laut in a difficult position. They need to define the limits of their economic relations so as not to endanger their social relations. In many respects, the Malays face the same problems in dealing with their kin as customers (Mariam Mohd. Ali, 1984:161-2; McKinley, 1981). Like the Malays, the Orang Laut do not want to make profits at the expense of their kinspeople. Exchanges between kin should therefore be things given, shared, or at the very most bartered to establish a bond between the transactors. It is the usual practice for the Orang Laut to *tukar* (barter exchange) things between themselves within their communities. An Orang Laut explained how things are circulated in his community.

Halus:
Yang Gaybang *tukar*ed her house with Siti Payong. This was because each of them wanted to relocate to where the other had already sited her house. By exchanging their houses, neither of them had to dismantle her house in order to use the wood for rebuilding elsewhere. The only thing that Yang Gaybang took with her was her door. We often *tukar* our boats with each other too. Bolong and Boat *tukar*ed their boats. Lacet and Awang Bai *tukar*ed their boats. Jais and Niam also *tukar*ed their boats. After that, Jais *tukar*ed his boat with Lampong. [Initially,] Lampong wanted to sell his *jokong* (a type of boat) for Rp. 15,000. However, since Jais wanted Lampong's boat, Lampong took Rp. 5,000 and one prawn spear from Jais. As for Den, he *tukar*ed his boat, a watch, and some money for a bigger boat with another sibling of his in Pulau Nanga.

Again, we are reminded that the Orang Laut use the word '*tukar*' or 'barter exchange' rather than the word '*jual*' or 'sell' for their exchanges. Parallels can be drawn with Smedal's (1989) discussion of the word '*tukor*' among the Orang Lom of Bangka, West Indonesia. According to Smedal (1989:186-7),

> [The Orang Lom] categorically (i.e., linguistically) [separate] two modes of exchange; viz. sale (*jual*) and barter (*toker*), of which the differentiating characteristic is not whether or not money is part of the transaction but how the actors approach one another, i.e. how money is contextualised. The difference between the two modes of money employment lies in the presence of a standard; i.e., a set price for a set weight. Thus, in the exchange (*toker*) mode I approach, money in hand, someone with a stock of rice. I show him my money, he presents some rice, and we may or may not agree to exchange. This is not selling. Selling, as the *Lom* conceptualise it, implies that the offer is constant, as it were; that buyers with the requisite amount of cash will be able to buy – whoever they are and whatever is the nature and content of their relationship. *Toker*, on the other hand, implies that the parties in the transaction are free to define the trading situation as they wish; if I don't like you I am not obliged to *toker* with you. *Toker*, therefore, depends on 'the meeting of two wishes' (*kepingin sama kepingin*). It is tempting to compare this to the difference between on the one hand sex between two people desiring each other and, on the other, sex as a commercialised service. In the latter case the vendor (the prostitute) cannot reasonably refuse his or her client (all the latter is expected to do is to fulfil his/her part of the contract: to pay); in the former the mutual attraction obviates or negates the category of the client.

Barter must be understood in the light of its social context. As the context varies, so will the features of barter itself (Humphrey and Hugh-Jones, 1992:2; Needham, 1975). Barter exchanges among the Orang Laut differ slightly from those of the Orang Lom. The Orang Laut incorporate the notion of money into their barter exchanges where necessary or appropriate. For them, the focus of barter exchange is on the demand for certain things or services, which can be either similar or different in kind. Boats and houses are either directly bartered one for the other, or for an assortment of other things such as watches, fishing spears, and even money.

The use of money in barter exchange within the community does not impose any set standards. An Orang Laut involved in barter exchange does not see the use of money as alienating the thing from its previous owner. Rather, it can be said that the very use of money is socially constructed. In other words, social relationships within the community shape the meaning of money. Below is an example illustrating how the use of money is perceived within the Orang Laut community of Tiang Wang Kang, Batam.

> Muay:
> Naomi's mother wove these rattan baskets. You can easily buy bamboo-woven baskets on the market. However, you can never find rattan baskets at the market. Rattan baskets are sturdier. I do not know how to weave them, but Naomi's mother is very skilled at weaving them. She will not sell her baskets, but she will make them for us if we ask her. She does not tell us a fixed price for them. Instead, we use our common sense and think of things to *tukar* with her. A lot of work is involved in making these baskets. First of all, she has to enter the jungle to look for rattan. That takes time and hard work. When she brought me the baskets that I had asked for, I gave her some rice, sugar, and money in return. At other times, I may give soap or some other things with a bit of money. She would not like it if I made it like a payment and gave her only money. I usually include some other things. The money is not to pay her. It is to help her. After all, we know that we are all poor here.

The Orang Laut do not see the use of money in barter exchange as payment. Instead, it is perceived as 'helping' the other member of the community who has, in the first place, agreed to 'help' by exchanging their resources. Although there are no set prices for things exchanged, money is sometimes used in addition to other things to make what the Orang Laut consider a fair exchange.

> Suri:
> Sometimes we use money when we barter because we do not want to *rugi* (come out short). Just think, if one of my brothers with a bigger boat were to exchange his boat for a smaller boat belonging to another brother of mine, my brother with the bigger boat would lose out. Therefore, sometimes, we add a little money to equalize the exchange.

The use of money balances a barter exchange. It is not intended for one member to profit from the other. The transactors in choosing barter as their form of exchange desire to establish a bond between themselves. Money may be contextualized as strengthening the bond by either rendering help or giving the other a fair exchange. This means that not everyone possessing money is able to obtain whatever he desires without regard to the relationship between the transactors. The willingness to barter with one another depends upon the already existing relationship between the transactors.

Although barter exchanges consist of mutual payments, which theoretically conclude a transaction, the transactors often engage in further barter exchanges with each other at a later time. Unlike a selling transaction, a barter exchange can involve the two parts of a transaction occurring simultaneously or separated in time. That is, a barter exchange can be a one-off transaction whereby the transactors pay each other off immediately. However, it can also be broken into two parts whereby the recipient's payments are considerably delayed in time. The element of trust that the obligation will be met eventually and the building of strong social relations in barter trading are thus of paramount importance (Humphrey and Hugh-Jones, 1992:8-9).

Ceco was unable to build his new house over the sea on his own. He called in his brother-in-law Tekong, a man known for his construction skills, to help him. In this exchange, neither Ceco nor Tekong expected to pay or to be paid in terms of money. This is because both men maintained that they were *ipar* (brothers-in-law). Nevertheless, when the house was finally completed, Ceco slipped some *uang kopi* (coffee money) to Tekong for his services. Ceco acknowledged that the money he had given to Tekong was only a fraction of what Tekong would have received if he had built a similar house for someone else beyond their community. Nor did Tekong ask for more. Ceco further explained that the money he had given Tekong was merely a token establishing an unspoken understanding with Tekong that he would render Tekong his skills or services at some future time when needed. Tekong did not object to this as Ceco is a much sought after *dukun* in his community.

The relationship between the transactors engaged in barter exchange is prolonged by the possibility of delayed payment. When this time element enters, the idea of trustworthiness during the waiting period can be interpreted in two ways. First, the transactors must trust that mutual payment will be made in due course (Humphrey and Hugh-Jones, 1992:8-9). Second, the transactors must trust that neither will manipulate or harm the other via the thing or skill that has been exchanged. In this case, Tekong could have either cast a spell on the house that he had built, or deliberately constructed it incorrectly to facilitate the entry of evil spirits.

The use of money in Orang Laut inter-community exchanges also blurs the neat categorization of bartering, giving, and selling as separate types of exchanges (Humphrey and Hugh-Jones, 1992). Below are examples of this overlap.

1. The minimum cost of calling in the midwife services of Suri, an Orang Laut in Pulau Nanga, consists of approximately Rp. 20,000, a new set of clothes, a piece of new *sarong* material, and a chicken. The customary package of a threaded needle stuck in a coconut, a candle, tamarind, salt, and lime for the midwife after the delivery of the baby has also to be included. However, when delivering the babies of her siblings and sisters-in-law, Suri would usually only take Rp. 20,000 and a threaded needle stuck in a coconut plus a candle, forgoing the chicken, *pulot* (glutinous rice), and clothes. It is said that as long as one is not stingy with her, Suri will reciprocate by rendering her *ilmu* as a midwife without the extra charges. Suri is even willing to deliver babies for members of her community who cannot afford any immediate payment other than a promise that they would reciprocate in some form or another at a later date if she should need any of their resources. In such cases, just the customary package is sufficient.

2. When the woman of a family is unable to row the boat for her husband as he concentrates on spearing fish, the couple will ask a child from the community to be a rowing partner for the trip. This is usually the case when the couple does not have any children of their own old enough to perform this task. After such trips, it is an unspoken understanding that the child should be given some money from the sale of the catch -- because they 'have worked together -- in addition to some other snacks that the couple buy from their Chinese *thau-ke*. If the couple should fail to give the child anything, they would come under heavy criticism from other adult members of the community. They would also not receive further help from the community in the future.

These examples show the ambiguity involved in distinguishing the concepts of giving, bartering, and selling (Humphrey and Hugh-Jones, 1992:6). This ambiguity is intentional as it allows the articulation of a bargaining process without making it so obvious as to hinder the establishment of a bond between the transactors.

The focus of the foregoing has been on how value is endowed, enhanced, or redefined in things such as food, boats, fishing spears, hand-woven rattan baskets, and even skills and services through specific modes of circulation within Orang Laut communities. To sum up, what we have seen is 'the network of social relations of obligations ... which is more powerful, better provisioned and more secure than atomised individual households' (Sneath, 1993:204). Most important of all, this network is the key in demarcating a symbolic load of insider versus outsider relations, and hence strengthening Orang Laut group solidarity and identity.

NOTES

1. The Orang Laut's obligation to share almost parallels that of the Semai, the aboriginal Malays of Malaysia. The latter have to 'share' whatever surplus food they can afford. If the Semai have 'only a little surplus over [their] immediate needs, [they] share it with [their] nuclear family; if more, with people in [their] house or neighbouring houses; if a large amount, with all the people in [their] settlement' (Dentan, 1979:49).
2. Lacet had become infected after visiting a prostitute in Tanjung Pinang.
3. Siti-payong is Lacet's sister-in-law.
4. Den is Lacet's older brother. Den is also Ross's stepfather. Ross's mother, Yang, married Den after Ross's biological father died.
5. Ceco is Lacet's older brother.
6. Endi was suffering from intestinal worms.
7. There are slight variations in this between different households. However, for all of them, the hundredth day after the death of the person is undisputedly the day to host the *kenduri besar*.
8. This is a Chinese cake, which the Malays do not use in their *kenduri*. This particular cake does not contain any pork. Nevertheless, in their feasts the Orang Laut sometimes serve other Chinese cakes that contain pork.
9. The Orang Laut's adoption of me as one of them was also expressed in their giving me some of their family heirlooms. I have discussed this in the previous chapter in the section on inalienable family heirlooms.
10. The incorporation of a person marrying into the community is also often expressed and declared via a marriage *kenduri* in which the couple and the community eat together. This is also the case with Malay marriage *kenduri*s.
11. The Muslim Malays consider drinking alcohol a sin.
12. The attempt to Islamize by a number of Orang Laut is not in contradiction with their non-attendance at the *kenduri* hosted by the Malays to mark their solidarity at the start of the *Hari Raya Puasa* celebrations. Wee (1985) supports this view in her analysis of the hierarchies of being Malay in Riau when she states that the aspiration of the Orang Laut in converting to Islam is to belong to a larger

cosmopolitan Islamic *umat* (congregation), rather than to the local community of Islamic Malays.

CHAPTER 7

MONEY:
RECONSTRUCTING THE MEANING OF THINGS

Picture 7: The tray of payment for Suri's services

Money, and the use of it by the Orang Laut, has symbolically blurred all traditional boundaries separating people as 'pure' versus 'impure' Malays in the Malay World. Correspondingly, it has symbolically freed them from positions of authority versus subordination in the Malay hierarchy. The Malays consider those Orang Laut who use money 'more modern and progressive' than those who do not. What the use of money does at the point of transactions between these two groups is to reconstruct their identities by redefining the spatial and temporal context of the interaction. The use of money re-situates them in the modern market economy as opposed to the hierarchical Malay World. These reconstructions enable them to 'interact safely,' as the basis of the interaction now rests upon the extent of the Orang Laut's economic rather than supernatural power. Certain features of money have made these reconstructions possible. As Hart (1986:638-9) aptly says:

> Look at a coin ... One side is 'heads' – the symbol of the political authority which minted the coin; on the other side is 'tails' – the precise specification of the amount the coin is worth as payment in exchange. One side reminds us that states underwrite currencies and that money is originally a relation between persons in society, a token perhaps. The other reveals the coin as a thing, capable of entering into definite relations with other things, as a quantitative ratio independent of the persons engaged in any particular transaction ... The coin has two sides for a good reason – both are indispensable. Money is thus at the same time an aspect of relations between persons, and a thing detached from persons.

The logic of money as a commodity is bound up with anonymous markets. Although it is about relations between people in society, money is also something which is able to enter into definite and quantitative relations with other things independent of the persons engaged in the transaction. On the one hand, money operates as a standard of value and unit of account with quantifiable and definite values (Humphrey and Hugh-Jones, 1992:8) and, on the other, things are quantified to represent a certain amount of money for exchange purposes (Neale, 1976:8). This means that when money is used in a transaction, contracts of exchange can be fulfilled immediately with no further obligations between the transactors.

This chapter begins with Orang Laut accounts of how they first became familiar with money as a medium of exchange. They regard the Chinese merchants and middlemen as the prime movers in their transition towards a monetized economy. The Chinese as leaders of diverse money-making enterprises in Riau represent an alternative way of becoming progressive without becoming Malay. Equally important is that the Chinese also represent an inversion of power in Riau. While the Chinese encourage the Orang Laut towards a monetized economy to avoid the practical inconveniences of barter trading, the Malays avoid barter trading with the Orang Laut for fear of establishing social relationships with them. For similar reasons, barter trading is avoided between different groups of Orang Laut themselves. Yet the use of money coupled with barter exchange has redefined things and services, thus enabling everyone across boundaries to interact, touch, and obtain these services and things safely.[1] This freedom stems from the perception that the use of money depersonalizes things and interactions, hence curtailing the fear of being poisoned through personalized non-monetary exchanges. Also, the use of money restructures the meaning of things and skills by redefining the social contexts in which the exchange takes place. For the Malays and the Orang Laut, the alienation or distancing of persons from things and skills involved in a transaction and from the transaction itself is an indispensable feature of exchanges using money. Thus the use of money has facilitated interaction between the different groups of Orang Laut, but also between the Malays and the Orang Laut.

Money

Money in the form of paper notes and minted coins has only recently become the main currency for trade by the Orang Laut. However, there are those who continue to feel that money has no place in their fishing activities.

> Bego:
> If we take money with us while we are out fishing, we will not be able to catch any fish. If we leave our money behind with our women, we will be able to have a good catch.[2] Our grandparents taught us this. This has been passed down from our ancestors.

For the Orang Laut like Bego, the presence of money in their fishing voyages would only court misfortune. Nevertheless, this does not mean that Bego considers it useless to have money. He was merely stressing the need to keep his maritime activities apart from monetary transactions. On the other hand, there are Orang Laut who do acknowledge their ancestors' teachings, but admit a more relaxed attitude towards carrying money on their fishing voyages. The use and perception of money among the different groups of Orang Laut still vary a great deal throughout Riau. Nevertheless, in whichever way money has penetrated lives, it has been a catalyst in the transformation of identity. By and large, the non-Orang Laut communities, especially the Malays, do not associate the Orang Laut with a monetized economy. They regard those Orang Laut who 'use money' as 'more progressive, modern, and clever' than those who 'still' practise barter only. In fact, the use of money among the Orang Laut is so recent that many still remember how they first came into contact with money as a medium of exchange.

> Imah:
> Formerly, we did not use *uang* (money). We had enough to eat, so we simply *tukar barang* (exchanged things). It was through our Chinese *thau-ke*s (bosses) that we first learnt to use money. In the past, there were no motorized boats. We often rowed our *thau-ke*s' goods to Singapore and back again. During these trips, we learnt through observation the ways in which the Chinese used money. We began to know the value of money and started using it too.

The Chinese have been traders involved in a long and close relationship with the Orang Laut, and in the course of time have owed much to the skills of the Orang Laut in expanding their business networks within and beyond the Archipelago. It was the Chinese who taught the value and use of money to the Orang Laut who, in turn, quite naturally view the Chinese as the prime movers in steering them away from a barter trading economy. An Orang Laut explained his *thau-ke*'s preference for a monetized economy.

> Boat:
> Acuk would rather give us money when we bring our fish to him.[3] He says he gets confused when his shop becomes crowded. He is afraid of getting cheated. The Malays will always plan to enter his shop at the same time with the intention of confusing and cheating Acuk. However, it is not us who cheat Acuk. So, Acuk would rather settle [with money] the fish that we bring to him immediately. Then, we go around his shop to buy what we need with the money that he has given us. Whatever money is left is ours for us to use later.

The *thau-ke*s have confirmed such reasons for their preference for using money over barter exchange. A former *thau-ke*'s wife recalls the transition from barter trading to using money with the Orang Laut.

> Mrs. Cou:
> During the time when Acuk's father and I were running the shop, the Orang Laut did not want money for their fish. Instead, I had to give them food and coffee each time they came in with their fish. I had to

keep cooking and brewing coffee in great quantities all the time. As you know, there are no fixed times for catching fish. They came in at all times. Sometimes they would want other things. I cannot understand why, but the Orang Laut were not interested in money then. Now it is much easier. You can settle their fish with money immediately. These days, it is much easier for Acuk's wife. It is also less confusing, especially when the shop is crowded. (Translated from Teochiu)

Although the Chinese are directing the Orang Laut towards a monetized economy, both groups recognize that the use of money has also created other difficulties.[4] On some occasions, the Orang Laut simply do not have ready cash, or they do not attach any value to what cash they have.[5] The first problem will be discussed in a later section on the system of credit that the *thau-ke*s have set up both for the Orang Laut and the Malays. With regard to the question of value, although the Orang Laut are aware of the strength of some other foreign currencies such as the Singaporean dollar against the Indonesian *rupiah*, they also speak of the uselessness of possessing such money in Indonesia.

Sman:
Ai is my *thau-ke* in Singapore for g*amat* and *nabi*.[6] Many of us will row directly to Pasir Panjang, Singapore[7] if we have as much as 20 to 30 kilograms of *gamat* and *nabi*. The Singapore Chinese *thau-ke*s also buy smoked rubber sheets and tin-ore from Indonesians. They used to buy turtles too.[8] It is the Chinese and not the Malays who know how to eat turtles, *gamat*, and *nabi*. The Chinese also want the teeth of the *duyong* (sea cow) for medicinal purposes.

The *thau-ke*s in Singapore give us a lot of money for these things. Here in the islands, the *thau-ke*s give us less money; it is like playing a child's game. Therefore, we do not get many things from our *thau-ke*s here. There [in Singapore], we can get garlic, shallots, new clothes or gunny sacks of second-hand clothes, good quality rice, sugar, gold, radios, television sets, motors, and all sorts of other things for our *gamat* and *nabi*. Once I bought a sack of second-hand clothes weighing 70 kilograms for only [Singapore]$15. Each piece was only about 30 [Singapore] cents. Our *thau-ke*s give us Singapore dollars for our *gamat* and *nabi*. We know that the Singapore dollar is good, but it is useless for us to bring it back. Therefore, we *tukar* (exchange) it for clothes, gold, and all sorts of things. We can do all this within [the restricted area of] Pasir Panjang. We do not want to bring any Singapore dollars back. Our purpose in going to Singapore is to exchange our *gamat* and *nabi* for these things which are all very cheap. Pasir Panjang is a bustling place. Our Singapore *thau-ke*s are very good to us. They will always give us a packed meal – sometimes of rice and sardines – when they know that we are leaving.

The trading station in Singapore is dominated by Chinese *thau-ke*s. This raises two significant issues. First, the Chinese recognize the importance of setting up shops for things like garlic, clothes, and mechanical gadgets within the restricted trading centre for the convenience of the Orang Laut. This is a solution to problems that arise from a solely monetized economy. It is a means to help the Orang Laut to conduct what they describe as 'exchanges' for their 'useless cash.' Second, the dominance of the Chinese in this trading scene reinforces the perceptions of the Orang Laut and the Malays of Riau that the Chinese are a trading community with extensive networks beyond the Malay World. For the Orang Laut and Malays, the Chinese represent another order of power and social structure.

In drawing the Orang Laut into a monetized economy, the Chinese have also introduced several ideas about money. Money in the form of paper notes and minted coins is non-perishable; money is a commodity which cannot be directly consumed; and money represents specific amounts of stored value which serve as a resource for future purchases or payments (Enzig, 1966:314). By this means, it is made known to the Orang Laut that anyone possessing money has the means to enter into the orbit of markets at any time in the present or future (Neale, 1976). This has significant implications for the relationships between the Orang Laut and the Malays. In possession of money, they feel more assured of having the freedom to carry out non-personalized and thus relatively safer transactions across their boundaries as and when they wish.

Many Orang Laut are able to recollect the various currencies that have been used in conjunction with different periods of political domination in Riau.

> Imah:
> In my lifetime [in the Riau Archipelago], I have used five different types of money. It started with the *uang dollar* (the dollar), followed by four others. I cannot remember [their order], but there was one which had the *cap burung* (seal of a bird), another which *pakai layah* (was stamped with a sail), and now it is the *rupiah*.

The Orang Laut explain that a change in the type of currency used often indicates a change in the central political body that is issuing it. For the Orang Laut, there is thus the understanding that money is a symbol of an over-arching political authority (Hart, 1986). Presently, the Orang Laut even speak of the exchange value of different currencies. They compare the value of the current Indonesian *rupiah* with other past and present world currencies that have been used in Riau.

> Buntut:
> The present Indonesian *rupiah* is *tak pakai* (useless). We need several thousand *rupiah* to buy anything. In the past [in Riau], we used the Singapore dollar.[9] With just one cent, we could buy a lot of things. The period of the Dutch was good too. Their money was powerful. We could get lots of things with a little money. However, the Japanese were *jahat*. That was the most frightening and difficult time. Even with money, we could not get anything. During the Japanese occupation, all of us – it did not matter whether we were Orang Laut, Malay, or Chinese – underwent similar sufferings.

In discussions concerning the use of money, the Orang Laut speak of everyone – 'whether Orang Laut, Malay, or Chinese' – in Riau on equal terms. This is because money functions as a token of trust guaranteed by a central power (Simmel, 1978:177). Even the aristocrat Malays recognize that in such a context, the central power is no longer vested in them. Instead, it pivots around an 'external criterion' (Humphrey and Hugh-Jones, 1992:8) – such as the Dutch, the Japanese, and the Republic of Indonesia – to represent the community. This is a significant shift from the way in which relationships in non-monetary exchanges are contextualized. Relationships were then seen in terms of ranks structured by the era of the Sultan.

BARTER AND MONEY

Notwithstanding the importance of a monetized economy and the attempts by the Chinese to orientate the Orang Laut towards such an economy, barter also continues in Riau. There are relevant issues that can be drawn from Humphrey and Hugh-Jones's (1992:2-6) discussions of barter. Unlike the use of money, barter is an institution of trade, which can and does exist within many kinds of wider political relations and between different types of society. Unlike the symbolism in the use of money, there is no external or over-arching institution to act as a guarantor of trust for the participants. Barter enables its own social relations to exist in a wide range of situations. It is also able to coexist with other forms of exchange, such as gift giving. As such, the strategies and obligations in one sphere often spill across into others. The characteristics of barter itself therefore enable it to be a viable form of exchange between the Orang Laut and Chinese. However, these are precisely also the features which account for the Malays' preference for engaging in a monetized economy rather than a strict barter exchange economy with the Orang Laut.

The Malays want to avoid direct exchange of things and services with the Orang Laut. Although barter is supposed to be separable from other forms of exchange, there are no hard and fast boundaries between them. Barter in one or another of its varied forms often coexists or is linked with other forms of exchange and shares some of their characteristics. Accordingly, social relationships are not always clearly defined. Furthermore, transactions in barter may be separated or drawn out in time, and the Malays and Orang Laut do not desire any such on-going relationships between themselves (Humphrey and Hugh-Jones, 1992:2). The Malays criticize the Orang Laut for practising barter and try to avoid engaging in strict barter trading, but they have not totally ceased using this form of exchange. This is so even though the Malays clearly favour a monetized economy that gives them a safe basis for exchange with the Orang Laut. The same can be said for the Orang Laut when they engage in inter-group exchange and with the Malays. The coexistence of barter trading and a monetized economy is not unique. As observed by Humphrey and Hugh-Jones (1992:6), 'there are few if any whole economies of any sizeable scale which are known to have operated by barter alone.'

The use of money in Riau has therefore enabled the Orang Laut and Malays to circulate things and services with more ease across their group boundaries. Parallels can be drawn with Parry and Bloch's (1991) study of how money is able to serve as an instrument of freedom in expanding the circle of trust in interactional patterns to provide wider social integration. However, Parry and Bloch have not extended their argument to stress the common aim in gift-giving, barter, and commodity exchange. Here, I adopt Hart's (1986:648) view that these different forms of exchange form 'a routinized resolution of social ambivalence' to secure 'the same ends, namely circulation of commodities between independent communities.'

'DOING BUSINESS' WITH THE CHINESE

The Orang Laut have a closer relationship with the Chinese than with the Malays. Both the Orang Laut and the Malays view the Chinese as a distinct group involved in but not part of the Malay World. The Chinese are referred to as '*Orang Tionghoa*' (*Tionghoa*: China) and/or '*Orang Cina*.'[10] This means a person from China but, to be more precise, the Orang Laut sometimes use the term '*peranakan pulau*' (an islander of mixed origins) to refer to those Chinese who were born in one of the islands of the Archipelago, or '*anak* Indonesia' (child of Indonesia), which can mean either a local or a foreign born Chinese who is residing in Indonesia permanently.[11]

The Orang Laut have often pointed out that because the Chinese are not *asli Melayu* (native Malays), it is 'safe' to interact with them. The Chinese are seen as a neutral and non-threatening group. The Malays see the Chinese neither as possessing *ilmu hitam* nor as having any interest in acquiring it to harm others.[12] The Chinese are believed to be keen only on moneymaking enterprises.[13]

State policies[14] and, to some extent, the Chinese community's own structural persistence, have perpetuated their separateness within the Malay World.[15] The state of Indonesia has differentiated the Chinese as an 'alien population.'[16] This has led to policies curtailing the economic, political, and cultural strength of the local Chinese.[17] Various Indonesian governments have maintained that their intention in weakening the Chinese community is to assimilate them into the indigenous society. However, many regulations in these policies contradict the declared assimilationist principles,[18] thus perpetuating the 'separateness' of the Chinese (Suryadinata, 1986:192).

There are many Chinese scattered throughout the Riau Archipelago. However, in May 1959, Chinese retail trade in rural areas was banned and they were forced to transfer their businesses to Indonesian citizens by 30 September 1959. At the same time no Chinese was allowed to reside outside certain designated administrative centres such as Tanjung Pinang, the township of Riau.[19] The forced migration of the Chinese to Tanjung Pinang further polarized the duality of *kampung* (village) and *kota* (town): indigenous and non-indigenous people (Wee, 1985:54).

The villages were and are still largely inhabited by the indigenes of Riau. This is in contrast to the towns, which are inhabited by the non-indigenes, such as the Chinese. The awareness of this duality is clearly indicated by language usage. Town dwellers speak *Bahasa Indonesia*, the Indonesian national language. However, 'one speaks the linguistically unstandardized and officially unrecognized dialect of the place in the villages' (Wee, 1985:54-5). The Orang Laut and Malays have often told me that a Chinese is an *orang kota* (town dweller). For those in Riau, Tanjung Pinang is therefore seen as the centre for the Chinese.

As state policies stipulate that the Chinese are not eligible for positions in the Indonesian civil service, many in Riau have been forced into setting up their own businesses. Furthermore, these policies have forced many Chinese to be outwardly oriented in their business practice. Some have involved themselves in smuggling activities;[20] others have looked to the patronage of

Singapore merchants to supply them with goods on credit or initial capital to set up businesses as middlemen in Riau (Ng, 1976:41).[21]

As middlemen, the Chinese in Riau connect the Orang Laut from the isolated areas in the Archipelago, the primary producers of maritime products and charcoal, to the big cities beyond the Malay World.[22] Conversely, they also facilitate the movement of consumer goods from the cities beyond the Archipelago to the producers. In so doing, they move between social groups and link the people in isolated areas to distant markets. In the role of middleman, they have also become the *thau-ke*s of the Orang Laut and the Malays. They keep accounts of the transactions and, for their trusted clients, they arrange a system of credit. An Orang Laut explains the working of such a system.

> Tekong:
> The *thau-ke* keeps a book. We take our fish to him and he writes the amount in his book. This is to redress whatever we owe him. Then, we can take *belachan* (shrimp paste), rice, sugar, chillies, and cigarettes from his shop. The next time we take our fish to him, he will open his book and the same thing happens. Sometimes we do not have any fish to give him. If he knows us well, he will help us. We can take the things from his shop first. However, if we have any fish, we must take them to him and not to any other *thau-ke*. Otherwise, if our *thau-ke* finds out, he will be angry and will not help us in future.

The credit system works on 'the equilibrium exchange ratios' based on the principle of trust (Anderlini and Sabourian, 1992:90). Still, the *thau-ke*s have set up a system to enforce or ensure that the system functions in a manner they desire. This is done through a verbal agreement that those who have received a middleman's '*bantu*' (help) must remain loyal to him and return to pay off the debts thus incurred with their maritime products or face future sanctions against receiving his help. Like middlemen elsewhere, they manipulate the prices of the maritime products received and the consumer goods paid out so that they keep their clients permanently in debt.

State policies seem to indicate a presupposition that the Chinese in Indonesia are politically oriented or show allegiance towards external political entities. Whether or not this is justified, the foreign orientation of the Chinese in their business practices has certainly contributed to shaping the view of the Malays and the Orang Laut that the Chinese are involved in, but not a part of the Malay World. For them, the Chinese are a group with peripheral status but have come to dominate the economic realm of Indonesia. In fact, the Chinese have brought about an inversion of power in the Archipelago by relocating, so to speak, the Malay World into a wider global market economy where status and power structures become redefined. It is interesting to note that the Malays and the Orang Laut alike now see themselves as the *anak buah* (followers/underlings) of the Chinese.

The Chinese have clearly adapted to various changes (Wang, 1990). They have seized every opportunity to improve their economic standing. This is evidenced by the numerous moneymaking enterprises they have embarked upon in spite of many periods of hostile government policies. They have even widened their trading partners to include members of the indigenous population of Riau regardless of their social standing. The Chinese believe that, although they are not Malays, their permanent residence in the region means that they are in fact a part of the Malay World. This has increased their vulnerability to being poisoned by either the Malays or the Orang Laut. As merchants in the region, they consider it necessary to interact closely with both groups of people.

> Su Lang:
> We believe that the Malays and the Orang Laut can poison us too if we provoke them. However, when we take their fish from them, we are doing business with them. They will not poison us when they sell their fish. Nonetheless, when they give us cakes or anything, we throw them away when they are out of sight. We are afraid of being poisoned. (Translated from Teochiu)

The Chinese reason that the use of money in the exchange of things and services changes the transactions into 'business' or 'business-like' activities. Such exchanges are regarded as safe because of the understanding that the things and services thus exchanged become commoditized. The things are thus neutralized from their previous identities and/or connections – a fact which decreases the possibility of them being used as instruments for poisoning. The moral overtones in using money, or in the calculation of exchanges in monetary terms, imply the immediate fulfilment or conclusion of the contract of exchange (Humphrey and Hugh-Jones, 1992:8; Neale, 1976:8). The Chinese believe that people place themselves on neutral grounds when they engage in 'business' for profit making purposes. There is thus no longer means of or motivation for poisoning. Things circulating as gifts beyond this monetized sphere are of course considered dangerous. Knowing that safe interactions can be made with the Malays and Orang Laut through 'business' and other employer-employee arrangements, the Chinese have monopolized many businesses: ice-making, snacks, boat building and repairs, tailoring, and hairdressing.[23] It is fairly common for the Chinese to employ the Malays or Orang Laut as domestic helpers, and even to engage their midwife services. In fact, the Chinese find it more convenient to employ the Orang Laut as domestic helpers because they are able to touch pork. They are also able to share the same meals with their Chinese employers. On religious feast days, some Chinese *thau-ke*s also give their surplus food to the Orang Laut who are in their employment. The Orang Laut interpret the handing out of food by the Chinese as acts of 'giving,' 'helping,' and 'generosity.' The Orang Laut who have been recipients of such things from the Chinese thus claim a closer allegiance with the Chinese than the Malays. In the course of my fieldwork, no Chinese was ever accused by the Orang Laut of poisoning anyone. They are of the opinion that Chinese *thau-ke*s are 'richer and more generous, less stingy, less fussy, and more willing to help' than their Malay counterparts.[24] Not surprisingly, many would prefer working for the Chinese, even though not all *thau-ke*s are equally generous and easy to work with.

Saya:
When I deliver babies for the Chinese, they give me lots of things. For example, when I delivered Asim's children, I asked for Rp. 20,000, a piece of cloth, and a set of new clothes. Instead, he doubled the payment because he pitied me. He even added sugar, coffee, and rice on top of Rp. 30,000. That is what he gave me for each child. When the child reached a month old, he gave me some more things. The Chinese are like that. They are not selfish. Not the Malays though.

The Chinese consider all their clients and employees to be their *anak buah* (followers/underlings). Wang (1990:15-16) explains that it is difficult for a single Chinese entrepreneur to start a business abroad without some degree of family backing. Therefore, the overseas Chinese merchants often enter a business by 'belonging to a family or an adopted family business network, including artificial brotherhoods operating as members under family discipline. This was fundamental even though it was less obvious abroad [to an outsider] that their business organizations had strong family characteristics.' Typically, if a Chinese *thau-ke*-employee relationship was close enough, the employee would be promoted rapidly in the business or even married into the family for a lifetime partnership. In other words, there were cases in which family relationships were synonymous with business relationships. If the relationship was less close, then the employees displaying industry would remain as 'loyal retainers all their lives' (Wang, 1990:16). To this very day, the Chinese merchants continue to maintain aspects of this *thau-ke*-employee relationship. On the Lunar New Year most Chinese *thau-ke*s give goodwill hampers to their *anak buah*. A red piece of paper or a red envelope symbolizing good luck and good fortune is always attached to the hampers. The Malays and the Orang Laut readily accept these hampers without fear of being poisoned. This act of giving and the symbolic red paper confirm and reinforce a firm relationship between the *thau-ke* and his *anak buah*. The Orang Laut are thus able to establish a type of relationship through 'doing business' with the Chinese which would be difficult to attain with the Malays. The following is an example of how some Orang Laut have been able to form strong *anak buah-thau-ke* relationships with the Chinese.

> Awang Ketah:
> If you are lucky and find yourself a good and helpful *thau-ke*, you will lead a s*enang* (contented) life. I was the first to settle in Dapur Enam. When my *thau-ke* asked me, 'Why don't you find yourself a wife?' I replied, 'I do not have enough money.' He answered, 'I will take care of everything.' So, I went and found a wife. When I married my first wife, he gave me everything – chicken, pork, money, rings, a few nights of *joget* (dance) – because I had worked hard for him. We feasted from morning till night for three days. When my first wife died, my *thau-ke* gave me $200 to cover all burial expenses.
>
> When I married my second wife, my *thau-ke* provided everything again. That *thau-ke* was the best. It was not as if he would pay me every time I brought my catch to him. Instead, there was an understanding that whenever my *thau-ke* was in any kind of difficulty, such as when thieves broke into his house, I would help him. Likewise, when my children or I were in any kind of difficulty and needed money – at that time we used Singapore dollars – he would give it. Later, when we used the *rupiah*, and I needed thousands of *rupiah* for my children, my *thau-ke* would help too. My *thau-ke* would also give us food whenever we had nothing to eat. During Chinese New Year, he would give us *ang pao*s (red envelopes containing money). When my *thau-ke* and his wife died, my sons and I dug their graves and helped carry their coffins for burial. I cried.

As seen above, an *anak buah-thau-ke* relationship may become so strong that it borders on enlisting the Orang Laut employee as a member of the 'family business network' (Wang, 1990). Below is an example of how a loyal Orang Laut was adopted and later made a *thau-ke* by his Chinese *bapak angkat* (adopted father). Chung Chai Hak was an immigrant from China who settled and worked in the charcoal kilns in Tiang Wang Kang. One day he adopted an Orang Laut boy whom he named Atong.[25] Atong's parents had also done short-term work in the kilns there, once from 1957 to 1958 and again in April 1962. On such occasions, Atong would invariably rejoin his parents. In August 1962 he married and has since settled in Tiang

Wang Kang. According to Atong, it was Chung who persuaded him to stay and work there.

> Atong:
> My adopted father was getting old. He wanted me close to him because he said that there was no one else to take care of him. Actually, although my adopted father was our *thau-ke*, he was in fact only the Headman of the charcoal kiln here. As far as my memory goes, the first *thau-ke*'s name was Lim Tuang, a Chinese Singaporean. During the period of the Confrontation, no Chinese was allowed to own any property in Indonesia. My adopted father Chung Chai Hak, who held the ownership documents for the charcoal kilns, made over the property in my name. That is how I came to own the charcoal kilns. Lim Tuang, the first *thau-ke,* raised no objection. Neither did Lim Tuang's younger brother Xiao Ti. My Chinese adopted father died on 12 April 1974. That was when he gave me all his possessions including the papers of ownership for the charcoal kilns.

The example above is an instance in which an Orang Laut *anak buah* was taken as part of the *thau-ke*'s 'family.' The political turmoil, which Atong outlined to explain how he came to be in possession of the kilns, highlights two important aspects of the Chinese community in the eyes of the Orang Laut. First, hostile government policies aimed at the Chinese community serve as constant reminders to the indigenes of the Malay World that the Chinese are not Malay; and, second, the 'alien' status of the Chinese *thau-ke*s compels them to collaborate with their *anak buah* in business arrangements.[26] The resultant close relationship between the Orang Laut and the Chinese has therefore led many Orang Laut to consider themselves 'united with the Chinese.'

> Bego:
> The Malays here pretend to be our friends. Actually, they are always looking for opportunities to harm us … The Chinese here are good. We are united with them. I have seen the Chinese being poisoned by drinks offered to them by the Malays … We are afraid of the Malays, but we like the Chinese.

> Awang Ketah:
> I have had to help *jampi* many Chinese who have been poisoned by the Malays here. However, I will never help the Malays.

Sman:
When I go fishing, I take my own food and water. Otherwise, I will ask for water from a Chinese, but never from a Malay. The Malays are *jahat* and *busok* (evil and smelly).

The Orang Laut see their alliance to the Chinese as a partial safeguard against the threat from a common enemy, the Malays. The Malays do not feel so close to the Chinese, even though, like the Orang Laut, they have never accused the Chinese of being obsessed with *ilmu*. The two communities may have different views of the Chinese; it is significant that both readily regard the Chinese as a neutral community in the Malay World. As such, the Chinese are viewed as intermediaries performing the important function of adding social distance to (hence neutralizing and making safe) things which then become acceptable for transaction between the polarized communities. Through the act of using money, the Chinese are circulating things and services into a different 'regime of value' (Appadurai, 1995:4).

Fish bearing marks of the spear are believed by the Malays to have been caught by the Orang Laut. For fear of being poisoned, no Malay would accept such fish as gifts. Yet, it is considered 'all right' for them to buy such fish from Chinese *thau-ke*s who have purchased them from the Orang Laut. As long as things, such as maritime products from the Orang Laut, have passed through the hands of the Chinese middlemen, they are considered safe to touch and even to consume. There is no longer fear of the fish containing poison. The Malays may still not be very keen to buy such fish. This is not a case of fear of poison; the Malays simply believe that such fish are 'smelly because the Orang Laut relieve themselves in their boats.' The Malays say that since the Singaporeans find it safe to import and consume maritime products from the Chinese, it must be 'all right' for them to do so too. It is also not uncommon for the Orang Laut to make *kajang*[27] (woven leaves) and collect shellfish for sale to the Chinese middlemen.[28] Once again, the Malays consider it safe to purchase such things from the Chinese. They prefer obtaining these things via the Chinese to approaching the Orang Laut directly. In the course of my fieldwork, no Malay has ever spoken of such things being poisoned.

'MAKING SAFE' INTERACTIONS BETWEEN DIFFERENT GROUPS OF ORANG LAUT

Different groups of Orang Laut view each other with intense suspicion and fear of being poisoned and harmed. They avoid giving and accepting gifts from each other. But the use of money has enabled them to redefine certain services and things so that they are able to interact safely between different groups.[29] The Orang Laut of Pulau Nanga and those of Teluk Nipah are examples of two conflicting groups who view each other with much fear and suspicion. Interaction between them is kept to a minimum. Individuals rarely issue invitations to weddings and funerals from one group to the other.[30] Yet, members of each group deem it necessary to seek *ilmu* and other services from the other.

Lampong, an Orang Laut from Pulau Nanga, was left a widower after the death of his wife Siti. His son could not be consoled over the loss of his mother. This caused Lampong endless anxiety over his son's health. Finally, the father decided that he would seek a *dukun*'s help to cast a spell on his son. It was a well-known fact among the Orang Laut that Pak Bujang, an elderly Orang Laut from the opposite island of Teluk Nipah, possessed the *ilmu* that Lampong needed to have his son 'cured.' Lampong explained why he had to cross over to seek Pak Bujang's help.

Lampong:
Pak Bujang casts very powerful spells to enable children to forget their deceased parents ... so that the children will be healthy again. People specialize in different kinds of spells. I paid Pak Bujang Rp. 25,000 and gave him a chicken to spell my son. That is why my son is healthy now. That was a lot of money, but it does not matter as long as my son is healthy.

The Orang Laut consider their *ilmu* to be an inalienable possession. What is transacted in all circumstances is not the content of the *ilmu*, but only the act of casting the spell. The *dukun*s will never recite aloud the content of their *ilmu*. The content will always be kept secret.

All the Orang Laut whom I talked to expressed great fear of being bewitched by members of a conflicting group. Therefore, it is very unusual that Lampong had the courage to approach a member of a different group to cast a spell on his son. The use of money in his case redefined the moral overtones of Pak Bujang's act of spell casting. It was transformed into a commoditized service that could be exchanged safely.

In a reversed situation, Meen's family from Teluk Nipah had on two occasions to seek Suri's *ilmu* as a midwife to deliver the babies of their daughters. Suri is the only midwife available to the Orang Laut in Teluk Nipah and Pulau Nanga.[31] When the second occasion arrived, the relationship between these two families had become extremely strained because of an unfortunate incident sometime before. Meen had engaged the service of Suri's husband Tekong to help him build a new house, but matters did not proceed as planned and the two sides harboured ill feelings against each other. However, the grudges were masked with much cordiality for fear of being poisoned. Soon after the quarrel, Meen's family found themselves in the dilemma of having to depend on Suri to deliver the baby of one of Meen's stepdaughters. The Orang Laut believe that a successful delivery rests upon the midwife's *ilmu*. There was therefore much fear in Meen's family that Suri might use her *ilmu* during the delivery to harm the mother and the baby. Meen explained the need to keep close watch on Suri during the delivery. He also stressed the need to practise their own *ilmu* in conjunction with Suri's for extra protection. Meen prepared and cast spells on the herbal medicine which he had prepared for this occasion. In addition, he cast more spells over his stepdaughter to protect her life. The reasons for these measures were never mentioned in front of Suri. Meen's family feared that if they provoked her in any way, she could poison them. On the other hand, Suri feared that her family, too, would be poisoned if she refused to deliver Meen's step-grandchild. Before rowing over to render her service, Suri gave strict instructions to her children not to accept anything from Meen's family.

Prior to the delivery, Meen's daughter and son-in-law visited Suri. They placed Rp. 20,000 as *uang muka* (money up front or down payment) in front of her. Suri was then successful in negotiating for a package of a set of new clothes, a new *sarong*, a kilogram of rice, a bottle of perfumed oil, a piece of soap, a chicken, a threaded needle stuck into a coconut, a candle, tamarind, salt, and a lime upon the delivery of the baby.[32] Suri explained that her acceptance of the money in advance meant that she was sealing a promise to be in close proximity during the period when the delivery was expected to take place. During the delivery, it was discovered that the baby's umbilical cord was wrapped dangerously around its neck. However, Suri was able to perform the delivery safely. Meen's wife Yang explained the added cost that this incurred.

> Yang:
> We had to give Suri another Rp. 10,000 because the umbilical cord of the baby was wrapped around its neck. This was not natural. The child could have died. Suri managed to save the child with her *ilmu*, so we had to add on a set of clothes and a piece of cloth for her. Prior to this, we gave her Rp. 20,000 as money in advance. She asked for all this. Formerly, my sister-in-law was a midwife too. However, she never asked for anything. She simply accepted whatever we gave her. She was different from Suri. We had to give Suri everything ... a chicken, a set of clothes, a piece of cloth. We spent about Rp. 50,000. She is a *nenek duit* (a money-grabbing grandmother) who eats money.

At the end of everything, we also gave Suri and the child yellow rice to *salamat* (give greetings of peace to) them.

The Orang Laut believe that in complications such as the above, it is only the power of a midwife's *ilmu* that can save both the mother and the child. Therefore, Suri had to cast even more powerful spells to rescue the mother and child from danger. The commoditization of the service of such a skill meant that this extra service commanded higher exchange value. Suri justified her position by explaining that if Meen's family had gone to a 'doctor' for the delivery, the latter would have asked for a higher fee.[33] She went on to say that she was like a 'doctor,' if not better.[34] Of course, the difference is that, unlike the 'doctor,' she used her *ilmu* to cast spells. Many Orang Laut believe that *ilmu* is even more powerful than medicine for delivering babies. Suri could therefore claim the right to be paid more. In giving her explanations for what had happened, Suri was clearly commoditizing her acts of spell casting as a service rendered.

The additional non-monetary items of payment that Suri had negotiated for had to be new and unused.[35] There are two explanations for this. Suri did not want to accept old things for her services; she would have felt short-changed. Also, Orang Laut from different communities avoid giving and receiving things that have had close association with their previous owners. It is a precaution taken to prevent the giver from poisoning the recipient through the thing. The things and money for this transaction with Suri were arranged on a tray for her. The money was visibly placed on top of everything. It was highly noticeable that Suri refused all other things not on the tray.[36]

In contrast to Yang's explanation of the patterns of exchange they were engaged in with Suri, Meen talked about the things that they had to give to those who had *tokang tulak* (skilfully pushed) the belly of his daughter during her contraction pains.

> Meen:
> After three days, the people who have pushed will be given half a kilo of pounded *beras* (uncooked rice grains). We have to pound the rice grains on our own. If we do not do this, we will fall ill. We will have to let those who pushed have a good look at the pounded rice grains. They will then rub it onto their hands and legs. If we do not give this to them, their hands and legs will be sick. It is not money that we will have to give the people who have pushed.

He explained that the skill of pushing rested upon the person's *ilmu*. It was not simply a matter of exerting pressure. Meen also pointed out that there was no need for him to give any money to the people who have helped to push, because they were his relatives in Teluk Nipah. Unlike the commoditization of Suri's services, Orang Laut belonging to the same community are expected to use their *ilmu* to help each other.[37] They trust their kin not to cast spells to harm or poison them.[38] While the commoditization of Suri's services led to a non-personalized bond between the transactors, exchange between members of the same Orang Laut community is usually aimed at creating lasting personalized bonds. Hence, the absence of money as a means of specific worth and payment indicates that it is 'help' and not a paid service that has been rendered. Although money is about relations between persons, it is simultaneously a thing detached from persons (Hart, 1986). It connotes definite and quantitative relations with other things independent of the persons engaged in the transaction. It is precisely this anonymity of persons that the Orang Laut are avoiding in their patterns of exchange with other members of their own community. In contrast, this is exactly the sort of relationship that the Orang Laut want to establish when they circulate things and services across their boundaries with other and perhaps conflicting groups.

'MAKING SAFE' INTERACTIONS BETWEEN THE ORANG LAUT AND THE MALAYS

The Orang Laut and Malay communities exercise much care in safeguarding themselves from being bewitched by each other's *ilmu*. However, much as the Malays fear the Orang Laut's *ilmu*, it is also this most powerful possession of the Orang Laut that the Malays desire.

In the course of my fieldwork, I had several opportunities to observe how the Orang Laut's casting of spells was transformed into a commoditized service which the Malays felt safe in obtaining. I was called upon to help out with negotiations in one such case.[39]

A Malay mother from Tanjung Pinang suspected that her son had been bewitched into falling in love with a girl from Pulau Tujoh.[40] Friends had informed the mother that the girl was an *ayam kampung* (lit. a village chicken, or used to mean a lady of pleasure) who had siphoned money off several men in exchange for her pleasures.[41] The girl was also said to have two other suitors from Pulau Tujoh. On many occasions, the mother had tried but failed to persuade her son to end the relationship. As time passed, the mother was told that her son was spending lavishly on the delights of his girlfriend, and that the couple was becoming increasingly intimate in public places. The mother exerted more pressure on him to 'see things rationally' and terminate the relationship. However, her son was determined to pursue the girl.

The mother finally decided to obtain an antidote from the Orang Laut to stop the affair. She regarded this as 'the only way' to correct the situation. The Malay woman drew me into her confidence. She reasoned that the only possible explanation for her 'usually obedient and shy son' turning against her and 'loving the girl to the point of insanity and without shame by displaying such intimacy under public scrutiny in broad daylight' was because the girl had bewitched him. To confirm her suspicion, the mother asked me if I remembered that her son had suddenly complained of feeling hot and had to unbutton his shirt earlier in the evening when it was raining heavily and was actually a very cold night. She went on to explain:

Ibu:[42]
Abang (older brother) displayed a definite symptom of having been bewitched when he complained of feeling hot earlier this evening. The rest of us were feeling cold. It was very unusual because *Abang* is always the first to complain of feeling cold. This is *malam jumat* (Thursday night/Friday early morning), the most powerful time for black magic to be carried out.[43] I am certain that the girl was at home casting spells on *Abang*. Poor *Abang*, we must save him quickly.

It is believed that while such spells are taking their effect, the victim acts out of the norm. This includes becoming irrational and suicidal. A great sense of discomfort is also felt, such as feeling hot or experiencing a burning sensation, throwing up, and choking. The mother believed that she could 'save' her son by obtaining a powerful antidote from the Orang Laut. I was asked to act on her behalf to negotiate with the Orang Laut for the antidote.

Following the mother's instructions, I started negotiations to obtain the antidote from Ceco, a well-known *dukun* on Pulau Nanga specializing in such matters. Ceco confirmed that he could cast spells and concoct an antidote to stop the girl from liking the boy and vice versa. The following conversation ensued on 8 December 1991:

Cynthia:
How much should *Ibu* pay you?

Ceco:
It is like this. She can give however much she likes.

Cynthia:
Ibu has said that she would only pay you if the spell works.

Ceco:
That is fine. She will know whether it works or not. If it works, and she does not give me anything, I can reverse the spell to harm her and the couple can get together again. Many people have come to me to cast spells for such matters. Recently, a Javanese sought me out to cast a spell on a girl whom he wanted. (At this point, Ceco took out several concoctions he had prepared for his various clients to show me.) Now, what you will need to do for your friend is to buy a bottle of *Minyak Wangi* (the name of a perfumed oil), and bring it back to me immediately.[44] I will cast a spell on the oil. After that, you will take it to your friend and ask her to massage it into her son's body. When the oil works, she will have to give me some tamarind, salt, and a nail. I will eat some of the tamarind and salt, and then you will have to take the nail and remaining tamarind and salt to her and ask her to eat them too. Let me know if the oil is not powerful enough. I will then prepare something more powerful. Ask *Ibu* to give me a packet of *Gudang Garam* (a brand of cigarette) too.

After Ceco concocted the antidote, he cautioned me to 'take [the oil] back safely,' and not spill any of it on myself. This would have resulted in me being bewitched instead. Although monetary payment for Ceco's antidote could be delayed until the potion proved effective, it was clear from Ceco's warning that he would reverse the spell and inflict harm on the recipients if he was not duly paid. The role that money plays in the exchange of things and services between the Malays and the Orang Laut can clearly be deduced from Ceco's caution. Monetary payment, once made, would mean an immediate fulfilment of a contract of exchange. The relationship between the Malay woman and Ceco would cease at that point and Ceco's potions and casting of spells would be transformed into commoditized services. Once these things are exchanged with money, they will no longer be identified with him. Instead, they will become the private or exclusive property and right of the Malay woman.

On 12 December 1991, I presented the Malay woman with the antidote, with which she later massaged her son. However, the antidote proved ineffective. Even after its application, the boy was still seen taking the girl out.[45] Three days later, I explained to Ceco the ineffectiveness of his antidote, whereupon he asked that I recount the details of the couple again. It was at the last meeting that the Malay woman told me the girl was from Pulau Tujoh.[46] When I added this to the previous information that I had already relayed to Ceco, he accused me of omitting a vital fact in my earlier account of the couple. He explained, 'People from Pulau Tujoh are very powerful in their *ilmu*.' He was therefore convinced that he would have to prepare a more powerful antidote. He also decided on another method of administering it.

Ceco:
I have to see the girl and boy in order to tell if it is the girl or the boy who wants the other. By looking into their eyes, I would be able to tell if the *hantu* (spirit) has entered them. I need to speak to the boy's mother. I have only cast the spell once so we cannot expect the *ilmu* to work immediately, because the girl has cast numerous spells many times over the boy. The longer you wait, the more this girl will cast spells until it will be too difficult to counter her spells. I have to cast spells several times now before it is too late.

There are several ways in which I can solve the problem. One is by massaging spellbound oil. I can also cast spells over water for the boy to bathe in or the food that he eats. However, you have to speak to his mother first because I have to know who will be there in the family who is going to eat the food. If you bathe in the water or eat the food that I have cast spells over, you will be harmed instead.

Ceco's willingness to meet the Malay woman to discuss the matter is in marked contrast to the usual avoidance of contact between the Orang Laut and the Malays. The use of money in this instance ensures social distance, hence safety from being poisoned through direct contact. Ceco suggested that if it was difficult for the Malay woman to travel to Pulau Nanga, he could go to Tanjung Pinang for four days to cast spells and prepare an array of potions until the boy was 'cured.' He explained that this was a complicated task which could not be accomplished in a day. He stated that the woman should give him money for the cost of his passage to Tanjung Pinang and for his food. Interestingly, he never once suggested that the woman give him food instead of money for food. Ceco's sister Suri came to join the discussion. She had been the person who had referred me to Ceco. It was not long before she started negotiating on behalf of her brother for the amount of money that the Malay woman should give Ceco for the antidote.

Cynthia:
How much will it cost?

Suri:
It is like this. *Abang* Ceco is too shy to say how much it would cost. *Ibu* will just give Rp. 20,000 to Ceco's wife before he goes, and another Rp. 20,000 to him later. That is Rp. 40,000 for four days. This

is to help feed Ceco's family while he is away from his fishing activities to help *Ibu*.

Cynthia:
Ibu is not very wealthy. Will Rp. 30,000 be acceptable?

Suri:
(Looking at Ceco.) She is asking for Rp. 30,000. (Pause.) *Abang* Ceco is a very skilled *dukun*. All sorts of people have come to him, and he has helped them in various ways – to get married, to break off relationships, or to bring a couple together again when they are on the verge of breaking up.

Cynthia:
I shall have to tell *Ibu* what you have just said, and I shall let you know of her opinion.

Ceco:
I will not speak to anyone else of this matter.

A few days after the above conversation, I conveyed Ceco's message to the Malay woman. Although she would have been pleased if Ceco had lowered his demands, she confided that she was willing to give however much the Orang Laut *dukun* asked. Even though the Malay woman was aware that Malay *dukun*s would have asked for less, she brushed aside all suggestions of obtaining alternative antidotes prepared by a Malay *dukun*. Four days later when I returned to Pulau Nanga, Ceco's wife Asmah approached me. The following discussion ensued.

Asmah:
How much is the Malay woman going to give Ceco?

Cynthia:
She will leave Rp. 10,000 for you first, and give him the rest when he gets to Tanjung Pinang.

Asmah:
He would be gone for a long time. Rp. 10,000 will not be enough for me to buy rice and food for the family when he is gone. Neither would it be enough for him to buy petrol for the boat to take him to Tanjung Pinang. Four days is a long time. Why does that Malay woman want him to be there for so long?[47]

Cynthia:
Because *Abang* Ceco himself said that he would need four days.

Ceco's wife, like his sister Suri, was insistent on bargaining with the Malay woman for more money in exchange for Ceco's services. This is yet another aspect of how conflicts between the Malays and the Orang Laut are resolved by the use of money: they interact to set a price for the circulation of their things and services. This is in contrast to their need to protect themselves by masking and suppressing all conflict at all other times. Both the Malays and the Orang Laut have often cautioned me that overt expressions of conflict could lead to the injured party feeling insulted and angered. This would be reason enough for the wrongdoer to be poisoned through the other's *ilmu.*

It was finally arranged with Ceco and the Malay woman that they would meet in Tanjung Pinang and negotiate directly. What happened in fact was that Ceco was unable to leave for Tanjung Pinang immediately. By the time he was able to, the Malay woman had, in her own words, 'slapped' her son 'across his face four times until he cried and repented.' In spite of having solved the problem in such a manner, she was still of the opinion that her son had been poisoned, but had 'fortunately been saved in time.' The Malay woman still believed in the power of Orang Laut *ilmu*, and with this case solved, wanted to seek Ceco's or any other powerful Orang Laut *dukun*'s *ilmu* to restore good working relations between another son of hers and his superior at the office.

The dealings between Ceco and the Malay woman are but an example of the symbolic power that money possesses. Their negotiations show how money is able to weave newly defined identities and social relationships between the Malays and Orang Laut so that both groups are able to interact to the extent of obtaining potions from one another with less fear of being poisoned.

TRANSFORMATIONS

The Orang Laut carry out various forms of exchange for the circulation of things and services within and beyond their community. Gift exchange coexists with barter trading and monetary transactions. The chosen forms of exchange are flexible according to variable conditions affecting the exchange and trading activities. The ways in which a thing or skill is exchanged endow different meanings to the item. Different social relationships are also established between the transactors in the exchange of such things and services. The various forms of exchange carried out by the Orang Laut can be considered as strategies and obligations to enable things and skills to enter and leave different spheres of social structure (Humphrey and Hugh-Jones, 1992:6).

In Chapter 1, I presented a modified version of Leach's idea (1989:40) on the metaphoric condensation of things to explain the system of social classification and symbolic boundaries affecting the Orang Laut in the Malay World. The foregoing discussion on how the Chinese middlemen have encouraged the Orang Laut towards a monetized economy suggests an additional formulation on the position and identity of the Orang Laut in relation to the Malays in Riau. The additional points are:

7. 'We' the Orang Laut and 'they' the Malays live within the same territory. All of us are destined to shared experiences.
8. Thus we share similar logical derivations from the following oppositions:

$$\frac{\text{Money}}{\text{Gift/barter exchange}} : \frac{\text{Modern market economy}}{\text{Malay kingdom}} :$$

$$\frac{\text{Civil society}}{\text{Concentric representation of power}} : \frac{\text{Ancestors no longer exist}}{\text{Ancestors exist}} :$$

$$\frac{\text{We are members of the civil society}}{\text{We are Malays versus Orang Laut}}$$

Money and markets are part of a global economy that is penetrating the lives of the Orang Laut. The ease with which the Orang Laut and the Malays have absorbed money and the modern market economy into their local conditions and economy adds an essential dimension to our search for an effective understanding of the forces shaping the modern world (see Hart, 1986). They have taken an institution foreign to them and made it their own. This has facilitated interaction across group boundaries. The use of money has thus allowed different groups to interact and transact on an equal basis. Simultaneously, the use of money has also inverted the power relationships in Riau. It has reconstructed the meaning of things and the identity of the Orang Laut.

NOTES

1 These include the services of healers, midwives, and house builders.
2 It is common for men and women to fish in pairs. The men usually do the spearing, while the women are responsible for rowing the boat. However, there are times when men and women go out fishing independently.
3 Acuk is the name of Boat's *thau-ke*.
4 Humphrey (1985) and Anderlini and Sabourian (1992) have shown that monetary exchange is not always better than barter, nor has the former necessarily evolved out of the latter.
5 This is also the case with the other communities, for example the Malays, the Javanese, and the Boyanese.
6 *Gamat* (*Echinocaulis*) and *nabi* are different species of sea cucumbers. *Nabi* is the more highly valued of the two.
7 This trading centre is also known as the Pasir Panjang Barter Trading Station in Singapore. It is a restricted area and is open only to Singaporeans with official entry passes. They, like the Orang Laut who may not possess any passports, are given temporary permits to trade within the restricted area for a stated number of hours. However, the Orang Laut, like many others who enter Singapore via Indonesian waters, face the frightening prospect of being arrested, jailed, and ill-treated by the Indonesian authorities for smuggling.
8 Present conservation laws which protect the diminishing turtle population have made it difficult for the Chinese *thau-ke*s to engage in the turtle trade with the Orang Laut.
9 The banking sector in Riau is still heavily dependent upon the money market of Singapore and Malaysia. In fact, the Singapore currency circulated in the Archipelago until about 1962 (Ng, 1976:9). The present-day import and export businesses of the Riau Chinese middlemen are carried out using Singapore currency. The middlemen maintain that the Singapore dollar in comparison with the Indonesian *rupiah* is more reliable, with less value fluctuation. It is a well-known fact that, among the islanders of the remote islands in the Archipelago, the only people with whom Singaporean currency may be exchanged are the Chinese *thau-ke*s.
10 Much controversy surrounds the designation of Indonesian Chinese as '*Orang Tionghua*' or '*Orang Cina*' (formerly spelt '*Tjina*'). In 1966, a top-level army seminar replaced the terms '*Tionghoa*' (Chinese) and '*Tiongkok*' (China) with the derogatory term '*Tjina*' (China and/or Chinese). The following was cited as one of the major reasons for the change: 'to remove a feeling of inferiority on the part of our people [indigenous Indonesians], while on the other hand removing the feeling

of superiority on the part of the group concerned [the local Chinese] within the states' (Coppel and Suryadinata, 1978:121). In January 1967, Major-General Sumitro, then Commander-in-Chief of Brawijaya, and later the Chief of Staff on the operational command for the restoration of security and order, urged the Chinese to accept the term '*Tjina*' because

> Indonesians of *Tjina* extraction are already in the big Indonesian family and have accepted the Indonesian culture ... We can no longer tolerate the existence of Chinese temples, nor can we tolerate *petilasan-petilasan* (traces) which smell Chinese. We will restore everything to *asli* [indigenous]. Do accept our measures ... Celebrations of Chinese New Year need not be continued, except by those Chinese who are aliens (*Berita Antara (edisi pagi)*, January 5, 1967).

By 25 July 1967, the Indonesian cabinet presidium decided to refer to the Chinese as '*Cina*' in all official documents. According to Suryadinata (1986:42-3), '*Cina*' is now used by most Indonesian newspapers.

11 There is much confusion over the term '*peranakan*' in the literature on Chinese in Indonesia. Most writers use it to refer to Indonesian-born Chinese, regardless of whether or not they use Indonesian or an Indonesian dialect as their daily language (see Coppel, 1973:143-7 for various meanings of '*peranakan* Chinese'). However, some writers (see Skinner, 1963; Suryadinata, 1986) use it in a stricter sense to include only Indonesian-born Chinese who do not have command of the Chinese language and speak only Indonesian. I do not intend to enter the debate on such terms. Instead, for the purpose of understanding how the Orang Laut perceive the Chinese, I am merely employing the term as used by the former. For the Orang Laut, the term '*peranakan*' refers to any Chinese who has lived in Indonesia for most of his or her life. This is regardless of the Chinese's ancestry and language fluency.

12 Although the Orang Laut claim that the Chinese have sought their help for *ilmu*, the former maintain that the sort of *ilmu* obtained by the Chinese, usually love potions, is merely for personal use, and not to harm others.

13 The majority of the Chinese are regarded as *thau-ke*s and economically better off, and as such unlikely to commit any evil or be thieves. During the course of my fieldwork, the authorities arrested a *thau-ke*. Reasons for the arrest were unclear. Some attributed it to the authorities accusing the *thau-ke* of possessing a motor without proper documents. Others said that it was due to the *thau-ke*'s smuggling in of sugar and rice from Singapore. More importantly, this was how the Orang Laut defended the *thau-ke*.

All [the authorities] want is money. The Chinese are never thieves. They are rich and can buy all the motors they need. They are not like the Malays or even some Orang Laut who steal. What is wrong with bringing in sugar and rice from Singapore? It costs less and they are trying to help us. The Chinese are good. It is the authorities who are bad!

14 In spite of the long presence of Chinese in Indonesia (Ng, 1976; Purcell, 1980), the *pribumi* (indigenous) leaders – a term used by the leaders themselves (Siddique and Suryadinata, 1982:67) – of the Republic of Indonesia still regard the Chinese as an 'alien population.' The leaders see the Chinese as an exclusive group dominating the Indonesian economy, but with links to China. The loyalty of the Chinese is therefore seen as oriented towards China, and away from Indonesia. Most of the leaders also view the Chinese as untrustworthy. They believe that in the past, the Chinese served the interests of colonial powers (Dutch and Japanese) (Suryadinata, 1986). It was also not until recently (see, for example, Mah, 1990; *Singapore Business*, 1990; Lee, 1990; H.L. Lee, 1991; Wong and Ng, 1991) that the prolonged business ties which the Chinese have had with Singapore laid them open to further suspicions and criticism by the *pribumi* leaders.

15 Before the 1950s, the Chinese community in Riau made numerous attempts at maintaining a separate group identity. For example, Ng (1976) records that it was through the Chinese patron-client clan relationship that new immigrants formed solidarities and found work in Riau. This relationship transplanted the gentry politics and power prevalent in Chinese villages to overseas Chinese communities. The Chinese elite also used the temples in Tanjung Pinang and Senggarang to create a centripetal force among the Chinese communities, and hence to establish their gentry power over the Chinese community in the nineteenth century. Another aspect of the community, which perpetuated their exclusiveness also, became prominent at the turn of the nineteenth century. This was when Riau became the economic frontier of Singapore (*ibid*:12). Tanjung Pinang, the township of the Archipelago, became a vibrant place of trade, and the Chinese began to centre their social activities there. Soon, this strengthened the position of the Hokkien merchants who dominated Tanjung Pinang. In 1910, the Chinese community also founded the Tuan Pun School in Tanjung Pinang to promote Chinese nationalism and the Chinese language. The Chinese written language was of immense practical value to the Chinese as it was the medium of communication in the commercial network of the Chinese middlemen. All Chinese storeowners in Tanjung

Pinang were expected to support the school or face a boycott of their stores (*ibid*:33-4).

16 According to Suryadinata (1986:191), the '*peranakan* Chinese' wanted to be regarded as one of the *pribumi suku* (indigenous groups), just like the Bataks, the Minangkabaus, the Balinese and other regional-indigenous-ethnic minorities. President Sukarno reluctantly accepted this view in the early 1960s. However, the majority of leaders objected to it. First, in their view, all indigenous ethnic minorities had particular regions to identify with. However, the Chinese minority was scattered around to the extent of being a 'floating urban minority.' Second, unlike indigenous minorities, the Chinese were said to have ties with one external power which was also their land of origin. Such views led to some Indonesian cities requiring citizens of Chinese origin to obtain special identity cards for security reasons (*Sinar Harapan*, 29 January and 20 February 1975; *Tempo*, 15 February 1975:18). In Jakarta, the Chinese are differentiated from other Indonesians by having the digit 0 placed at the beginning of their registration number (Wee, 1985:43). The re-categorization of indigenous and non-indigenous entrepreneurs has also reinforced the division between indigenous Indonesian and ethnic Chinese (Suryadinata, 1986:193).

17 In the economic field, the Benteng system in 1950 favoured indigenous importers over the Chinese. Regulations were implemented to indigenize harbour facilities and rice-mills by shifting the ownership of these things from the Chinese to indigenous Indonesians during the 1950s. Priority in issuing licences was given to new enterprises owned by indigenous Indonesians in 1954 and 1956. Foreign investors were required to collaborate with local firms in which indigenes were major share-holders in 1974, and certain loans were available only for indigenous businessmen in 1975 (Suryadinata, 1986:191). Examples of policies to curtail the political and cultural strength of the Chinese included 'the requirement that Indonesian citizens receive Indonesian education (1957), the ban on alien traders in rural areas (1959), the name-changing regulations for non-indigenous Indonesians (1961, 1967), the easing of the naturalization process (1969) [and] the closing of Chinese medium schools (1966)' (Suryadinata, 1986:191).

18 For example, the official re-adoption of the derogatory term '*Cina*' to refer to the Chinese has offended and alienated them further. The high expenses still necessary for the process of naturalization have furthermore deterred many Chinese from becoming Indonesian citizens. The policy of re-categorizing indigenous and non-indigenous Indonesians in economic activities, which has favoured only the indigenes, has prevented the assimilation of the Chinese (Suryadinata, 1986:192).

19 This situation was aggravated after the failed coup in 1965 when

...the overseas Chinese were held responsible for the alleged role of the [People's Republic of China] in the abortive Coup ... Regional authorities took independent action against them. For instance, the military authorities in early 1967 prohibited alien Chinese from trading in East Java and parts of Sumatra (Suryadinata, 1986:135).

20 Many Chinese businesses became involved in smuggling activities during the Confrontation between 1963 and 1966. This was due to state regulations which not only banned all their businesses (Ng, 1976:41), but also made it impossible for them to enter into the civil service. The high prices that Singapore offered for rubber and primary products drew many Chinese into smuggling activities. The possibility of accumulating foreign exchange abroad was another pulling factor (*ibid*:59). Smuggling became even more attractive during the Sukarno period when a system of strict foreign exchange control was implemented. Foreign exchange could then be traded on the black market at a rate ten times its official value (*Business News*, 24 March 1976:3). The Chinese used the profit on exchange for import capital. After the Confrontation between 1963 and 1966, there was extensive collaboration between Chinese merchants and state administrators in these smuggling activities (*Far Eastern Economic Review*, 1 June 1967:478).

21 The commercial ties between Singapore and Indonesia were so close that Singapore currency was used throughout Riau until the Confrontation started in 1963 (Ng, 1976:59). Riau had long been an extension of Singapore, and the Chinese businessmen in the region were criticized for being the commercial agents of Singapore (see for example, *Indonesian Current Affairs Translation Service Bulletin*, 1971:478).

22 The Orang Laut and non-Orang Laut chop the mangrove swamps to obtain charcoal. The charcoal is then exported to Europe.

23 Ice is needed for preserving fish.

24 This is especially so with reference to giving credit.

25 Atong is a Chinese name. It is also the name by which everyone calls this Orang Laut now.

26 According to a number of my informants, the Chinese have 'even married the Orang Laut' in an attempt to gain Indonesian citizenship.

27 These usually serve as rooftops for boats. Alternatively, they may be used as walls of houses and sheds or as mats for drying various maritime products.

28 Shellfish are gathered by hand. They do not bear any spear marks. Thus, it is much more difficult to identify the people who have collected them.

29 These include the services of healers, midwives, and house builders.
30 However, it is common for members of each group to cross over to gamble with each other.
31 There is a Malay midwife on the neighbouring island of Sembur. However, neither the Malay midwife nor the Orang Laut are keen to interact on such a basis. The Orang Laut from Teluk Nipah regard calling in Suri from the conflicting and different Orang Laut group of Pulau Nanga, rather than the Malay midwife, as the lesser of two evils. On the other hand, the Malay midwife is keen to distance herself from the Orang Laut. According to the Malays of Sembur, the midwife is afraid to deliver any Orang Laut's baby. Should complications arise during the delivery, the Orang Laut would accuse her of poisoning them. In such circumstances, the midwife would be vulnerable to being poisoned by the Orang Laut as a counterattack. The Malay midwife also regards the Orang Laut as a people having either a different religion or none at all. This would also complicate matters for her should either the mother or the baby die during the delivery. This is because she would not be able to assist in their burial and funeral rites in the expected role of a midwife.
32 The things that Suri had asked for are items traditionally – with occasional variations – requested by other Orang Laut and island Malay midwives. The Malay midwives, too, cast spells while carrying out a delivery.
33 By this, Suri meant a doctor in a hospital practising western medicine.
34 Both the Orang Laut and Malays told me of cases where *dukun*s were called into the hospital at Tanjung Pinang, the township of Riau, to work alongside the doctors. Although I was not personally acquainted with such cases, I was told these were cases in which the attending doctors could not manage the complications that had arisen during the delivery.
35 Although it is not a common practice to give a midwife old and used things, it is possible to do so if both sides are agreeable to such a transaction. However, the Orang Laut told me that this would be an exception rather than the norm, such as when one kin helps another.
36 Suri had tried not to show her refusal of things beyond the tray too visibly. She had also reminded her children to be polite and not to be too obvious in their refusal of offers of refreshments lest they too offend and provoke Meen's family into poisoning them.
37 Kinsfolk who do not help are sometimes accused of harbouring evil intentions to inflict harm. Tut, the sister of Meen's stepdaughter, was helping to push her sister's stomach during the delivery. All of a sudden, she sprang backwards and fell into a fit. Meen later confided in me that they knew who had inflicted harm on his family. They told me to recall how Buntut, the oldest woman in their community, who in spite of

possessing the most powerful *ilmu* in the community, had walked in and out of their daughter's house during the entire period of the delivery without attempting to help. For them, this was an indication that she was casting spells to harm Meen's stepdaughter. Because Meen was also casting spells to protect his stepdaughter from being poisoned. This then resulted in the evil spirit bouncing off onto Tut.

38 There have been cases in which relatives have been accused of poisoning one another. However, I observed that these accusations were often levelled at those who had married into the group. That is, these people had belonged to a conflicting group of Orang Laut prior to their marriage. For example, a few Orang Laut of Pulau Nanga whispered to me that their brother, Den, had married a *Suku Barok* (a sub-group of Orang Laut) woman. The Orang Laut of Pulau Nanga view the *Suku Barok* with suspicion. They believe that the *Suku Barok* woman had bewitched Den into marrying her. When the woman became their *ipar* ([sister]-in-law), she entered their community and lived amongst them. She was not able to have any children of her own and was therefore keen on adopting one of Den's brother's daughters. However, the parents of the girl, Ceco and Asmah, refused permission. On the day when Ceco's daughter drowned, the Orang Laut told me their sister-in-law had lured the girl into her home and given her food. They say that out of spite, their sister-in-law had cast spells on the food and poisoned the girl. This resulted in the girl feeling dizzy and falling into the sea. The Orang Laut whispered this story to me as they 'did not want anyone to hear, especially Den.' This was because the latter was their 'own brother.' They reasoned that it was after all not he who had done wrong, but his Suku Barok wife. Although the Orang Laut may accuse others within their own community of bewitching one another, care is taken even by the family claiming to have been victimized that such news should never reach the family of the accused. They fear this would cause divisions within the community.

39 I was called upon to mediate in the negotiations for two reasons. The first was due to the distance between the woman's residence in Tanjung Pinang and Pulau Nanga, the Orang Laut settlement where the woman had hoped to obtain the antidote. As I returned to Tanjung Pinang at the end of each month to collect my mail, I was seen as the ideal person who was in touch with both communities. Second, the woman trusted that because of my friendship with the Orang Laut, I would be able to recommend her a powerful Orang Laut *dukun*. This case clearly illustrates how a dangerous antidote could be transformed into a safe thing for the Malay woman to use (without being harmed). Prior to my establishing any contact with the Orang Laut, this woman had, out of great concern, been adamant that I should not associate with the Orang

Laut. She feared that the Orang Laut, by my simply touching any of them or their possessions, would bewitch me. Yet, in this case, she deemed that this dangerous antidote could be made safe for me to handle when transporting it from Pulau Nanga to Tanjung Pinang.

40 Pulau Tujoh (Seven Islands) is a group of seven islands in the Lingga area of the Riau Archipelago of Indonesia.

41 *Ayam kampung* literally means 'village chicken.' However, it is here used to mean 'a prostitute.'

42 *Ibu* means mother. However, it is also a term used to address (older) women.

43 *Malam jumat* means literally 'night Friday,' that is the (Thursday) night preceding Friday. For the Malays, Fridays begin from three in the afternoon on a Thursday. The Malays and the Orang Laut also know *Malam jumat* as *malam hantu* (night of the ghosts or spirits). This is therefore the most powerful period for practising black magic.

44 *Minyak Wangi* serves two purposes. It is used by the Malays for prayers, and it is used by the Orang Laut when they *jampi* (cast spells).

45 After buying the bottle of *Minyak Wangi*, I had personally brought it to Ceco to check if this was indeed the oil that he had asked for. However, a Malay woman and a Chinese woman who were also close friends of mine thought that this was the wrong oil for such a purpose. They maintained that the oil *Minyak Wangi* was to bewitch people into falling in love. Instead, they were of the opinion that the oils *Sedap Malam* and *Bunga Tanjung*, after having been spellbound, were more commonly used to cause hostility between a couple.

46 The Malays and Orang Laut believe that there are centres of relatively more and less powerful black magic in Riau. Hence, it was common knowledge among them that Pulau Tujoh, where the girl came from, was a powerful centre for black magic.

47 Asmah was unhappy that her husband had to remain in Tanjung Pinang for four days because whenever Ceco visited Tanjung Pinang, he would patronize the prostitutes there.

CHAPTER 8

REFLECTIONS AND CHALLENGES

Picture 8: Mooring for a break

In this book I have examined the different forms of exchange between the Orang Laut and non-Orang Laut in Riau and interpreted them as acts of communicating and negotiating group identities and boundaries. These exchanges carry implications for understanding the identity of the Orang Laut within the broader framework of the political and religious institutions of the Malay World. Society is not an absolute entity which exists to create exchange; rather, it is exchange that creates the bonds of society (Simmel, 1978:174-5). Society is, therefore, the synthesis of these relations.

Previous studies on the Orang Laut have concentrated on questions of their ethnic identity (see for example Lenhart, 1997; Sandbukt, 1982; Sather, 1998; Mariam Mohamed. Ali, 1984; Wee, 1985). Issues concerning the wider non-Orang Laut community's avoidance of interaction with, and acceptance of things from, the Orang Laut have only occasionally been mentioned. However, no study has focused on the Orang Laut's identity as engendered through the exchange of things. The narratives and ethnographic accounts in this book thus add a new dimension to how group identities and boundaries can be, and have been, negotiated, reinforced, or perpetuated through an array of exchanges between the Orang Laut and the Malays. The acquisition or avoidance of different types of material artefacts has significant implications. It reflects social relationships within a society and mirrors past and present points of differentiation and power relations between groups of people in a society. Hence, exchanges are, in real terms, also acts of communication. Alternatively put, exchange not only does something; it says something (Malinowski, 1922; Levi-Strauss, 1969; Leach, 1989:6).

I have outlined the social-historical framework for examining the levels and forms of exchange between the Orang Laut and the Malays in Riau, and have suggested that the notion of boundary needs to be reconsidered. The Malay aristocrats regard themselves as pure Malays. They have defined their Malay World in terms of centred positions and spaces of power, and have correlated their authority with a spiritual power that is guided by the principles of Islam. To maintain an ordered polity, all others are expected to uphold this centrist polity without challenge. What is more, the pure Malays have constructed ideas to outline the shape and meaning of the Malay World. These ideas have been codified by both verbal and non-verbal signs such as genealogical charts, religion, language, codes of conduct, physical appearance, and a sedentary as opposed to a nomadic lifestyle. These criteria have been created by the pure Malays to give sense to ethnic categories and have had important implications for different groups in the area. First, these categories underscore differences in what could otherwise have been regarded as a homogenous group of Malays. Second, social processes of exclusion from and incorporation into the Malay World are now issues of concern. Third, social relationships in the Malay World revolve around differences in ethnic status across boundaries.

The Malays generally accept the Orang Laut as indigenous people of the region, and some have even spoken of having a common origin with them. However, they have also stressed how the Orang Laut have departed from being part of the ordered Malay World. This is based on their perceptions of the Orang Laut's refusal to abandon a nomadic lifestyle and to adhere to the principles of Islam, which can only be observed if one leads a sedentary lifestyle. The Orang Laut, on the other hand, have defined their own conception of an alternative Malay World. They have asserted claims to possessing the most powerful *ilmu* which makes them capable of subverting the hierarchy of power upheld by the Malays. The Malays do not dispute the extent of this power, but believe the Orang Laut have derived this power from their allegiance to evil spirits and thus consider it illegitimate and evil. As the Malays fear this power, seeing it as diminishing their authority and threatening the Malay World, they are committed to subjugating it and incorporating the Orang Laut into their notion of an ordered Malay World. Attempts have been made to draw the Orang Laut towards the Islamic faith and a sedentary lifestyle. In a much less pronounced way, the Malays also believe that the Orang Laut's power can be of use to them. Therefore, some Malays have, in spite of their fear of the subversion of their power by the Orang Laut, even attempted to cross boundaries to obtain such power.

The basis of group boundaries for the Malays and the Orang Laut thus lies in their points of differentiation with respect to being Malay. The different ways in which purity, power, and authority are conceived and defined by the Malays and the Orang Laut constitute significant issues in their differentiation, hence group boundaries. They need to cross this hurdle of differentiation for the purpose of safely acquiring things and skills from each other. By converting ideas or mental perceptions of boundaries into material objects 'out there,' they have given these boundaries 'relative permanence' (Leach, 1989:37). This is basically why different types of things exist for the Orang Laut at all.

There exist indigenous categories of meaning and social value for things owned by or associated with the Orang Laut. An indigenous logic here links persons with things, and, in turn, underpins the Orang Laut's domains of kinship and exchange. The issue here is that the meaning or value of things like fishing spears, boats, pounders, and stones is not simply what their simple function represents, but lies in their further symbolic significance. As an example, I have shown how a pounder whose initial utility is for pounding things has taken on a different symbolic meaning through time. Through wear and tear, a hole in its base has made it into a family heirloom emdowed with supernatural powers. For the Orang Laut and the Malays, it is through the production, exchange, association, and consumption of these things that different relationships among people are established and sustained.

The exchange of things has relational implications, hence social consequences as to one's identity. While it is possible for the Orang Laut to exchange non-adopted things with other groups, the exchange of adopted things and the attempt to keep inalienable adopted things out of circulation are full of implications. The circulation of such things creates debts, bonds, or forced reciprocity which entail future exchanges whereby relationships are established and maintained. Exchanges of such things also bring together partners and even entire families, thus defining the boundaries of groups and communities.

It can be argued that the conversion of the indigenous logic of group boundaries into a permanent form is a way of translating mental concepts into visible markers of boundaries. This 'has been done by creating special material objects which serve as representations of the metaphysical ideas and their mental environment' (Leach, 1989:37).

The crossing of boundaries, just as much as the transition from one social status to another, calls for a ritual to bring about the transformation. This involves redefining the meaning of things through the introduction of money into the exchange practices in the Malay World. Elements of sociality are removed as things shift to the status of being commodities. Market relations have in a large way redefined the indigenous categorization and meaning of things. This has allowed some groups, such as the Malays, to acquire things which have either borne or been associated with the identity of the Orang Laut. I have brought my book to a tentative close by relating how contacts with a market economy constitute historically significant events – events which contribute fresh insights towards the reinterpretation of material culture, hence of identity.

GLOSSARY

abang	older brother
adat	proper behaviour, custom
adik	form of address to a younger sibling and younger people in an extended family, from a husband to wife, boyfriend to girlfriend, for service persons of either sex (waiter, etc.) younger than the speaker
agama	religion
Alam Melayu	Malay World
Amir al-mu'munin	Commander of the faithful
anak	child
anak buah	follower, underling
ang pao	red envelope containing money
asal	place of origin
asli	original, authentic
ayam kampung	lady of pleasure, prostitute (lit. a village chicken)
bahasa	language
bangsa	nation, people
bantu	help
barang	things
batin	chief
belachan	shrimp paste
beras	uncooked rice
besar	big
bomoh	practitioner of indigenous medicine
Bunga Tanjung	brand name of a fragrant oil
busok	smelly
cap burung	seal or inscription in the shape of a bird
cocok	to match harmoniously
daratan	mainland
daun t'rap	shredded tree bark
derajat	rank
dosa	sin
dukun	practitioner of indigenous medicine, shaman
duyong	sea cow
encik datuk	local chief

INDONESIAN SEA NOMADS

encik keturunan	person of honourable descent
gamat	type of sea cucumber
Gudang Garam	brand of cigarettes
hamba orang	branded indigene slaves owned by individuals
hamba raja	serfs
hantu	ghost, spirit
hantu laut	sea spirit
Hari Raya Haji	religious festival after the Islamic pilgrimage to Mecca
Hari Raya Puasa	religious festival after the Islamic fasting period
hati	heart, liver, mind
hitam	black
Ibu	term of respect for a woman
ikut	to follow
ilmu	learning, science, magic
ilmu hitam	black magic
iman	religious guide
indera	royal
ipar	in-law
jahat	evil
jampi	to cast a spell
jaring	type of fishing net
joget	dance
jokong	type of boat
jual	sell
kabupaten	district
kado	gift, present
kajang	movable sun shade made of palm thatch
kampung	village
Kantor Social	Social Office
kecamatan	sub-district
kenduri	religious feast
kepala	head
kepenghuluan	headmandom
kepulauan	archipelago [see pulau]
keramat, kramat	places endowed with supernatural power
keris	wavy double-bladed dagger
keturunan	descendant/descent
kong	to bewitch
kota	town
kubur	grave

kue baluh	small cake made of flour, eggs, and margarine
kue ku	rice cake with a filling of crushed mung beans
kue rokok	pastry rolled up to look like cigars, hence its name '*rokok*' or cigarettes
kuning	yellow
kunyit	yellow ginger, turmeric
lain	other
lari	to run away, elope
layah	sail
lesung	pounder
lokek	stingy, selfish, miserly
maju	progressive
makam	grave with supernatural powers
malam hantu	night of the ghosts or spirits
malam jumat	period from Thursday evening to Friday at dawn
malu	shy, bashful, embarrassed, ashamed
mas kawin	dowry
masuk	to enter
Melayu dagang	foreign Malays
merah	red
Minyak Wangi	brand name of a fragrant oil
nabi	type of sea cucumber
nenek duit	money-grabbing grandmother
nyawa	soul
obat	medicine
orang asli Melayu	indigenous Malay
orang biasa	commoner
orang Cina	a Chinese
orang dari luar	outsider
orang hamba	common slave
orang Islam	Muslim
orang kerahan	nobility's vassals
orang kita	us, insider
orang kota	town dweller
orang laut	sea people
orang Melayu	a Malay
orang suku laut	tribe of sea people
pakai	to wear, use
pelanduk	mouse-deer
perahu	type of boat
peranakan	a Chinese person of mixed origins

INDONESIAN SEA NOMADS

piara	to adopt
pribumi	indigenous
pukul	to strike, hit
pulau	island
pulot	glutinous rice
puteh	white
Qur'an	the Islamic Sacred Text
raja	prince
Raja Laut	King of the Sea
rakyat	populace, citizenry
ribu-ribu	an ivy-like creeping vine
roh, ruh	soul
rugi	to lose, come out short
sakti	sacred, divine, supernatural power
salamat	greetings of peace
sampan	a type of boat
sampok	to become polluted
Sedap Malam	brand name of a fragrant oil
sarong	sheath dress
semangat	soul
Serambi Mekah	Gateway to Mecca
siput	mollusc
suku Melayu asli	original Malay divisions
suku sampan	boat tribe
tak pakai	useless
tengku	prince
thau-ke	middleman
Tiong-hua, Tiong-hoa	China, Chinese
tokang tulak	to push skilfully
toker, tukar	to exchange, barter
tripang	sea cucumber
tuan said	descendant of the Prophet Muhammad
uang	money
uang kopi	tip or bribe (lit. coffee money)
uang muka	money up front, down payment
umat	nation of Islam, congregation of believers
wajik	cake made of glutinous rice and palm sugar

REFERENCES

Andaya, Barbara Watson (1997) 'Recreating a Vision: Daratan and Kepulauan in Historical Context,' in: Cynthia Chou and Will Derks (eds) *Riau in Transition. Bijdragen Tot de Taal-, Land- en Volkenkunde* 153, pp. 483-508.

Andaya, Barbara Watson and Leonard Y. Andaya (1982) *A History of Malaysia*. London: Macmillan Press.

Andaya, Leonard Y. (1975a) 'The Structure of Power in Seventeenth Century Johor,' in: Anthony Reid and Lance Castles (eds) *Pre-colonial State Systems in Southeast Asia: The Malay Peninsula, Sumatra, Bali-Lombok, South Celebes*. Kuala Lumpur: Malaysian Branch of the Royal Asiatic Society. Monograph 6, pp. 1-11.

– (1975b) *The Kingdom of Johor 1641-1728: Economic and Political Developments*. Kuala Lumpur: Oxford University Press.

Anderlini, Luca and Hamid Sabourian (1992) 'Some Notes on the Economics of Barter, Money and Credit,' in: Caroline Humphrey and Stephen Hugh-Jones (eds) *Barter, Exchange and Value: An Anthropological Approach*. Cambridge: Cambridge University Press, pp. 75-106.

Anderson, Benedict R. O'g (1972) 'The Idea of Power in Javanese Culture,' in: Claire Holt, Benedict R. O'g Anderson, and James Siegel (eds) *Culture and Politics in Indonesia*. Ithaca and London: Cornell University Press, pp. 1-70.

– (1990) *Imagined Communities: Reflections on the Origin and Spread of Nationalism*. London, New York: Verso.

Annadale, Nelson and Herbert C. Robinson (1904) *Fasciculi Malayenses: Anthropological and Zoological Results of an Expedition to Perak and the Siamese Malay States, 1901-1902; Anthropology, Part 2*. London: The University Press of Liverpool.

Appadurai, Arjun (ed.) (1995) *The Social Life of Things: Commodities in Cultural Perspective*. Cambridge: Cambridge University Press.

Aristotle (1962) *The Politics*. Harmondsworth: Penguin Books.

Armstrong, Jocelyn M. (1984) 'Elements of Ethnic Ranking in Urban Malay Society,' in: Tan Chee Beng (ed.) *Contributions to South-east Asian Ethnography*, 3, December. Singapore: Double-Six Press, pp. 28-45.

Bappeda dan Kantor Statistik Kabupaten Kepulauan Riau (1988) *Kepulauan Riau Dalam Angka 1987*. Tanjung Pinang.

– (1993) *Kepulauan Riau Dalam Angka 1992*. Tanjung Pinang.

Barth, Fredrik (ed.) (1969) *Ethnic Groups and Boundaries: The Social Organisation of Culture Difference*. Oslo: Universitetsforlaget.
Benjamin, Geoffrey (1989) 'Achievements and Gaps in *Orang Asli* Research,' in: Hood Salleh (ed.) *Akademika* 35, July. Kuala Lumpur: Penerbit Universiti Kebangsaan Malaysia, pp. 7-46.
Berita Antara (edisi pagi) (1967) 5 January. Jakarta.
Bodenhorn, Barbara (1988) 'Whales, Souls, Children and Other Things that are "Good to Share": Core Metaphors in a Contemporary Whaling Society,' *Cambridge Anthropology*, 13/1, pp.1-18.
– (1989) '*The Animals Come to Me, They Know I Share*': *Inupiaq Kinship, Changing Economic Relations and Enduring World Views on Alaska's North Slope.* Unpublished Ph.D. thesis, Cambridge.
– (1990) '"I'm Not the Great Hunter, My Wife Is": Inupiaq and Anthropological Models of Gender,' *Etudes/Inuit/Studies*, 14/1-2 Quebec, pp. 55-74.
Bottignolo, Bruno (1995) *Celebrations with the Sun: An Overview of Religious Phenomena among the Badjaos.* Quezon City: Ateneo de Manila University Press.
Brown, C.C. (1953) 'Sejarah Melayu or "Malay Annals",' *Journal of the Malayan Branch of the Royal Asiatic Society* 25/2-3, pp. 1-276.
Brown, Peter (1970) 'Sorcery, Demons and the Rise of Christianity From Late Antiquity into the Middle Ages,' in: Mary Douglas (ed.) *Witchcraft, Confessions and Accusations.* London: Tavistock Publications, pp. 17-46.
Business News (1976) 24 March. Jakarta, p. 3..
Carsten, Janet (1987) 'Analogues or Opposites: Household and Community in Pulau Langkawi, Malaysia,' in: Charles Macdonald (ed.) *De la Hutte au Palais: Sociétiés 'à Maison' en Asie du Sud-Est Insulaire.* Paris: CNRS, pp. 153-68.
– (1991) 'Children in Between: Fostering and the Process of Kinship in Pulau Langkawi, Malaysia,' *MAN: The Journal of the Royal Anthropological Institute*, 26/3, September, pp. 425-43.
Chaussonnet, Valerie (1988) 'Needles and Animals:Women's Magic,' in: William Fitzhugh and Aron Crowell (eds) *Crossroads of Continents: Cultures of Siberia and Alaska.* Washington, D.C.: Smithsonian Institution Press, pp. 209-26.
Chou, Cynthia (1995) 'Orang Laut Women in Riau: An Exploration of Difference and the Emblems of Status and Prestige,' *Indonesian Circle* 67, pp. 175-98.
– (1997) 'Contesting the Tenure of Territoriality: The Orang Suku Laut,' in: Cynthia Chou and Will Derks (eds) *Riau in Transition. Bijdragen Tot de Taal-, Land- en Volkenkunde* 153, pp. 605-29.

Colchester, Marcus (1986) 'Unity and Diversity: Indonesian Policy Towards Tribal Peoples,' *The Ecologist* 16-2/3, pp. 89-98.

Coppel, Charles (1973) 'Mapping the Peranakan Chinese in Indonesia,' in: *Papers in Far Eastern History* 8, September, p. 106. Department of Far Eastern History: The Australian National University.

Coppel, Charles and Leo Suryadinata (1978) 'The Use of the Terms "*Tjina*" and "*Tionghoa*" in Indonesia: A Historical Survey,' in: Leo Suryadinata (ed.) *The Chinese Minority in Indonesia: Seven Papers.* Singapore: Chopmen, pp. 113-28. First published in: *Far Eastern History* 2, September, pp. 97-118.

Cuisinier, Jeanne (1936) *Danses Magiques de Kelantan*. Paris: Institut D'Ethnologie.

Dentan, Robert Knox (1979) *The Semai: A Nonviolent People of Malaya*. Fieldwork Edition. New York: Holt, Rinehart and Winston.

Dobbin, Christine (1983) *Islamic Revivalism in a Changing Peasant Economy: Central Sumatra, 1784-1847*. London and Malmo: Curzon Press.

Douglas, Mary (1970) *Witchcraft, Confessions and Accusations*. London: Tavistock Publications.

– (1985) *Purity and Danger: An Analysis of the Concepts of Pollution and Taboo*. London: The University Press of Liverpool.

Dunn, F.L. and D.F. Dunn (1984) 'Maritime Adaptations and Exploitations of Marine Resources in Sundaic Southeast Asian Prehistory', in: Pieter van de Velde (ed.) *Prehistoric Indonesia: A Reader*. Dordrecht: Floris Publications, pp. 244-71.

Embree, B. (1973) *A Dictionary of Southern Min*. Hong Kong: Language Institute.

Endicott, Kirk M. (1979) *Batek Negrito Religion: The World-view and Rituals of a Hunting and Gathering People of Peninsular Malaysia*. Oxford: Oxford University Press.

– (1991) *An Analysis of Malay Magic*. Oxford: Oxford University Press.

Enzig, Paul (1966) *Primitive Money: In its Ethnological, Historical and Economic Aspects*. Oxford: Pergamon Press.

Errington, Shelly (1989) *Meaning and Power in a Southeast Asian Realm*. Princeton, New Jersey: Princeton University Press.

Evans-Pritchard, E.E. (1976) *Witchcraft, Oracles and Magic Among the Azande*. Oxford: Clarendon Press.

Far Eastern Economic Review (1967) 1 June, p. 478.

Farah, Caesar E. (1970) *Islam: Beliefs and Observances*. Woodbury: Barron's Educational Series.

The Federal Constitution of Malaysia. See Malaysia: *Federal Constitution* below.

Findlayson, G. and Thomas Stamford Raffles (1826) *A Mission to Siam and Hue*. Quoted from C.A. Gibson-Hill (1973) The Orang Laut of Singapore River and the Sampan Panjang, *Journal of the Malayan/Malaysian Branch of the Royal Asiatic Society* 25/1, pp. 161-75. Reprinted in *150th Anniversary of the Founding of Singapore. Journal of the Malayan/Malaysian Branch of the Royal Asiatic Society*, pp. 121-34.

Firth, Raymond (1959) *Economics of the New Zealand Maori*. Wellington: R.E. Owen, Government Printer.

Geertz, Clifford (1989) *Negara: The Theatre State in Nineteenth-century Bali*. Princeton, New Jersey: Princeton University Press.

Gibson-Hill, C.A. (1973) 'The Orang Laut of Singapore River and the Sampan Panjang,' *Journal of the Malayan/Malaysian Branch of the Royal Asiatic Society*, 25/1, pp. 161-74. Reprinted in *150th Anniversary of the Founding of Singapore, Journal of the Malayan/ Malaysian Branch of the Royal Asiatic Society*. Singapore: Times Printers Sdn. Bhd., pp. 121-34.

Gow, Peter (1991) *Of Mixed Blood: Kinship and History in Peruvian Amazonia*. Oxford: Clarendon Press.

Gudeman, Stephen (1986) *Economics as Culture: Models and Metaphors of Livelihood*. London: Routledge and Kegan Paul.

Gullick, J.M. (1988) *Indigenous Political Systems of Western Malaya*. London: The Athlone Press.

Hart, Keith (1986) 'Heads or Tails? Two Sides of the Coin,' *MAN: The Journal of the Royal Anthropological Institute* 21/4, December, pp. 637-56.

Hill, A.H. (Translator) (1973) 'The Founding of Singapore Described by "Munshi Abdullah",' *Journal of the Malayan/ Malaysian Branch of the Royal Asiatic Society*, 28/III, pp. 125-32. Reprinted in *150th Anniversary of the Founding of Singapore, Journal of the Malayan/ Malaysian Branch of the Royal Asiatic Society*. Singapore: Times Printers Sdn. Bhd., pp. 94-111.

Hobsbawm, Eric and Terence Ranger (eds) (1992) *The Invention of Tradition*. Cambridge: Cambridge University Press.

Humphrey, Caroline (1985) 'Barter and Economic Disintegration,' *MAN (N.S.): The Journal of the Royal Anthropological Institute* 20, pp. 48-72.

Humphrey, Caroline and Stephen Hugh-Jones (eds) (1992) *Barter, Exchange and Value: An Anthropological Approach*. Cambridge: Cambridge University Press.

Indonesian Current Affairs Translation Service Bulletin (1971).

Ivanoff, Jacques (1997) *The Moken: Sea-Gypsies of the Andaman Sea Post-war Chronicles*. Bangkok: White Lotus Co. Ltd.

Kähler, Hans (1960) *Ethnographische und linguistiche Studien über die Orang Darat, Orang Akit, Orang Laut und Orang Utan im Riau-Archipel und auf den Inseln an du Ostküste von Sumatra.* Berlin: Verlag von Dietrich Reimar.

Kato, Tsuyoshi (1984) 'Typology of Cultural and Econological Diversity in Riau,' in: Narifumi Maeda and Mattulada (eds) *Transformation of the Agricultural Landscape in Indonesia.* Kyoto: Center for Southeast Asian Studies, Kyoto University, pp. 3-60.

Keeler, Ward (1987) *Javanese Shadow Plays, Javanese Selves.* Princeton, New Jersey: Princeton University Press.

Krige, J.D. (1990) 'The Social Function of Witchcraft,' in: Max Marwick (ed.) *Witchcraft and Sorcery: Selected Readings.* London: Penguin Books, pp. 263-75.

Leach, Edmund (1961) *Rethinking Anthropology.* London: University of London, The Athlone Press.

– (1989) *Culture and Communication: The Logic by Which Symbols are Connected: An Introduction to the Use of Structuralist Analysis in Social Anthropology.* Cambridge: Cambridge University Press.

Lee, Hsien Loong. 1990. Speech by the Minister for Trade and Industry, and Second Minster for Defence (Services) at the Topping-up Ceremony of Batam Industrial Park. Singapore in: *Singapore Government Press Release No. 45/August 15-1/90/08/28.* Singapore: Media Division, Ministry of Information and the Arts.

– (1991) 'Southeast Asia in the 1990s: Challenges and Opportunities,' in: *Singapore Government Press Release No. 17/February 15-1/91/02/27.* Singapore: Media Division, Ministry of Information and the Arts.

Lee, Tsao Yuan (1991) 'A Singapore Perspective,' in: Lee Tsao Yuan (ed.) *Growth Triangle: The Johor-Singapore-Riau Experience.* Singapore: Institute for Southeast Asian Studies, pp. 1-36.

Lenhart, Lioba (1995) 'Recent Research on Southeast Asian Sea Nomads,' *Nomadic Peoples: Journal of the Commission on Nomadic Peoples* 36/37, pp. 245-60.

– (1997) 'Orang Suku Laut Ethnicity and Acculturation,' in: Cynthia Chou and Will Derks (eds) *Riau in Transition. Bijdragen Tot de Taal-, Land- en Volkenkunde* 153, pp. 577-604.

Levi-Strauss, Claude (1966) *The Savage Mind.* Chicago: University of Chicago Press.

– (1969) *The Elementary Structures of Kinship.* Translated by James Harle Bell and John Richard von Sturmer. Edited by Rodney Needham. Boston: Beacon Press.

– (1987) *Introduction to the Work of Marcel Mauss.* London: Routledge and Kegan Paul.

Logan, J.R. (1847a) 'The Ethnology of the Johor Archipelago,' *Journal of the Indian Archipelago and Eastern Asia* 1, pp. 336-40.
- (1847b) 'The Biduanda Kallang of the River Pulai in Johor,' *Journal of the Indian Archipelago and Eastern Asia* 1, pp. 299-307.
Lomnitz, L.A. (1977) *Networks and Marginality: Life in a Mexican Shantytown.* New York: Academic Press.
Lummer, Elke (1992) 'Spurensuche: Piraterie im Riau-Lingga-Archipel (1800-1850),' in: Fritz Schulze and Kurt Tauchmann (eds) *Kölner Beiträge aus Malaiologie und Ethnologie zu Ehren von Frau Professor Dr. Irene Hilgers-Hesse*, Bonn: Holos [Kölner Südostasien Studien 1). pp. 131-50.
Macleod, Scott and T.G. McGee (1996) 'The Singapore-Johore-Riau-Growth Triangle: An Emerging Extended Metropolitan Region,' in: Fu-chen Lo and Yue-man Yueng (eds) *Emerging World Cities in Pacific Asia*. Tokyo, New York, Paris: United Nations Press, pp. 417-64.
Mah, Bow Tan (1990) Speech by the Minister of State for Trade and Industry, Republic of Singapore at the Opening of the Indonesia-Singapore Joint Investment Promotion Seminar in Osaka and Tokyo, 10-12 December, in: *Singapore Government Press Release No. 07/-December 15-2.90.12/10*. Singapore: Media Division, Ministry of Information and the Arts.
Malaysia: Federal Constitution Incorporating All Amendments Up to 15th May 1981. Compiled in the Office of the Commissioner of Law Revision. Kuala Lumpur: Director General of National Printing.
Malinowski, Bronislaw (1922) *Argonauts of the Western Pacific*. New York: E.P. Dutton.
- (1966) *Crime and Custom in Savage Society*. London: Routledge and Kegan Paul.
Mari Pangestu (1991) 'An Indonesian Perspective,' in: Lee Tsao Yuan (ed.) *Growth Triangle: The Johor-Singapore-Riau Experience*. Singapore: Institute of Southeast Asian Studies.
Mariam Mohd. Ali. 1984. *Orang Baru and Orang Lama: Ways of Being Malay in Singapore's North Coast*. Singapore: Department of Sociology, National University of Singapore. Unpublished Academic Exercise.
Marwick, Max (ed.) (1990) *Witchcraft and Sorcery: Selected Readings*. London: Penguin Books.
Marx, Karl (1961) *Capital, Volume 1*. Moscow: Foreign Languages Publishing House.
Matheson, Virginia (1989) 'Pulau Penyengat: Nineteenth Century Islamic Centre of Riau,' *Archipel* 37. Paris: Published with the help of the

Centre National de la Recherche Scientifique and the Institut National des Langues et Civilisations Orientales, pp. 153-72.

Matheson, Virginia and Barbara Watson Andaya (trans. and eds) (1982) *The Precious Gift (Tuhfat al-Nafis): An Annotated Translation*. Kuala Lumpur: Oxford University Press. (See Raja Ali Haji ibn Ahmad below.)

Mauss, Marcel (1990) *The Gift: The Form and Reason for Exchange in Archaic Societies*. Translated by W.D. Halls. London: Routledge.

Mayer, Philip (1990) 'Witches,' in: Max Marwick (ed.) *Witchcraft and Sorcery Readings*. London: Penguin Books, pp. 54-70.

McKinley, Robert (1981) 'Cain and Abel on the Malay Peninsula,' in: Max Marshall (ed.) *Siblingship in Oceania: Studies in the Meaning of Kin Relations*. Ann Arbor: University of Michigan Press, pp. 335-88.

Miller, Daniel (1987) *Material Culture and Mass Consumption*. Oxford: Basil Blackwell.

Milner, A.C. (1981) 'Islam and Malay Kingship,' *Journal of the Royal Asiatic Society of Great Britain and Ireland*, pp. 46-70.

Mubyarto (1997) 'Riau: Progress and Poverty,' in: Cynthia Chou and Will Derks (eds) *Riau in Transition. Bijdragen Tot de Taal-, Land- en Volkenkunde* 153, pp. 542-56.

Nadel, S.F. (1990) 'Witchcraft in Four African Societies,' in: Max Marwick (ed.) *Witchcraft and Sorcery: Selected Readings*. London: Penguin Books, pp. 286-99.

Neale, Walter C. (1976) *Monies in Societies*. San Francisco: Chandler and Sharp Publishers, Inc.

Needham, R. (1975) 'Polythetic Classification: Convergence and Consequences,' *MAN: Journal of the Royal Anthropological Institute* 3, pp. 349-69.

Ng, Chin-Keong (1976) *The Chinese in Riau – A Community on an Unstable and Restrictive Frontier*. Singapore: Institute of Humanities and Social Sciences, Nanyang University.

Nimmo, H. Arlo (1972) *The Sea People of Sulu*. San Francisco: Chandler.

Normala Manap (1983) *Pulau Seking: Social History and an Ethnography*. Singapore: Department of Sociology, National University of Singapore. Unpublished Academic Exercise.

Okely, Judith (1983) *The Traveller-gypsies*. Cambridge: Cambridge University Press.

Pang, Keng Fong (1984) *The Malay Royals of Singapore*. Singapore: Department of Sociology, National University of Singapore. Unpublished Academic Exercise.

Parry, Jonathan (1986) 'The Gift, the Indian Gift and the "Indian Gift",' *MAN: The Journal of the Royal Anthropological Institute* 21/3, pp. 453-73.

Parry, Jonathan and Maurice Bloch (eds) (1991) *Money and the Morality of Exchange.* Cambridge: Cambridge University Press.

Pemerintah Daerah Tingkat I Riau. (1994) *Wajah Riau '94: Gambaran Hasil-hasil Pembangunan di Daerah Riau Selama Pelita V.*

Polanyi, Karl (1944) *The Great Transformation.* New York: Holt, Rinehart and Winston.

Purcell, Victor (1980) *The Chinese in Southeast Asia.* Kuala Lumpur: Oxford University Press.

Raja Ali Haji ibn Ahmad (1982) *The Precious Gift (Tufat al-Nafis).* Translated by Virginia Matheson and Barbara Watson Andaya. Kuala Lumpur: Oxford University Press.

Raja Hamza Yunus (1992) *Pulau Penyengat Indera Sakti.* Pekanbaru: Yayasan Membaca.

Richards, Audrey (1939) *Land, Labour and Diet in Northern Rhodesia.* London: Oxford University Press.

Ricklefs, M.C. (1981) *A History of Modern Indonesia c.1300 to the Present.* London: Macmillan.

Sahlins, Marshall (1974) *Stone Age Economics.* London: Tavistock Publications.

Sandbukt, Øyvind (1982) *Duano Littoral Fishing: Adaptive Strategies Within a Market Economy.* Cambridge, United Kingdom: Department of Social Anthropology, University of Cambridge. Unpublished Ph.D. thesis.

Sather, Clifford (1971) *Kinship and Domestic Relations among Bajau Laut of Northern Borneo.* Harvard University, Cambridge MA: Unpublished Ph.D. thesis.

– (1984) 'Sea and Shore People: Ethnicity and Ethnic Interaction in Southeastern Sabah,' in: Tan Chee Beng (ed.) *Contributions to Southeast Asian Ethnography* 3, December. Singapore: Double-Six Press, pp. 3-27.

– (1985) 'Boat Crews and Fishing Fleets: The Social Organization of Maritime Labour among the Bajau Laut of Southeastern Sabah,' in: Anthony R. Walker (ed.) *Contributions to Southeast Asian Ethnography* 4, August. Singapore: Double-Six Press, pp. 165-214.

– (1995) 'Sea Nomads and Rainforest Hunter-gatherers: Foraging Adaptations in the Indo-Malaysian Archipelago,' in: Peter Bellwood, James J. Fox and Darrell Tryon (eds) *The Austronesians: Historical and Comparative Perspectives.* Department of Anthropology, Research

School of Pacific and Asian Studies Publication. Canberra: Australian National University, pp. 229-68.
- (1997) *The Bajau Laut: Adaptation, History, and Fate in a Maritime Fishing Society of South-eastern Sabah*. Kuala Lumpur: Oxford University Press.
- (1998) 'Sea Nomads, Ethnicity, and Otherness: The Orang Suku Laut and Malay Identity in the Straits of Melaka,' *Suomen Antropologi* 2/1998, 23. *Vuosikerta* 23/2 (Oct. 1998), pp. 20-36.
- (1999) *The Orang Laut*. Academy of Social Sciences (AKASS) Heritage Paper Series, Occasional Paper No. 5. Penang: Academy of Social Sciences (AKASS).
Schot, J.G. (1882) 'De Battam Archipel,' *De Indische Gids* 4/2, pp. 161-88; 470-9.
- (1884) 'Het Stroomegebied der Kateman: Bijdrage tot de Kennis van Oost-Sumatra,' *Tijdschrift voor Indische Taal-, Land- en Volkenkunde* (TBG) 29, pp. 555-81.
Scott, James C. (1985) *Weapons of the Weak: Everyday Forms of Peasant Resistance*. New Haven: Yale University Press.
Siddique, S. and Leo Suryadinata (1982) 'Bumiputra and Pribumi: Economic Nationalism (Indigenism) in Malaysia and Indonesia,' *Pacific Affairs* 54/4, pp. 662-87.
Simmel, Georg (1978) *The Philosophy of Money*. London: Routledge.
Sinar Harapan, Jakarta (1975) 29 January, 20 February.
Singapore Business (1990) 'Riau: An Investor's Guide to the 3,000 Island Province,' 14 /12, December. Singapore.
Skeat, Walter William (1900) *Malay Magic: An Introduction to the Folklore and Popular Religion of the Malay Peninsular* (sic). London: Macmillan and Co., Ltd.
Skeat, Walter William and H.N. Ridley (1973) 'The Orang Laut of Singapore,' *Journal of the Straits Branch of the Royal Asiatic Society* 33, pp. 247-50. Reprinted in *150th Anniversary of the Founding of Singapore, Journal of the Malayan/ Malaysian Branch of the Royal Asiatic Society*. Singapore: Times Printers Sdn. Bhd., pp. 118-21.
Skinner, G. William (1963) 'The Chinese Minority,' in: Ruth T. McVey (ed.) *Indonesia*. New Haven: Yale University Southeast Asia Studies, pp. 97-117.
Smedal, Olaf H. (1989) *Order and Difference: An Ethnographic Study of Orang Lom of Bangka, West Indonesia*. Oslo Occasional Papers in Social Anthropology 19. Oslo: Department of Social Anthropology, University of Oslo.
Smith, Adam (1904) *An Inquiry into the Nature and Causes of the Wealth of Nations*. New York: Putnam's Sons.

Sneath, David (1993) 'Social Relations, Networks and Social Organisation in Post-Socialist Rural Mongolia,' *Nomadic Peoples*, 33, pp. 193-207.

Sopher, David E. (1977) *The Sea Nomads: A Study of the Maritime Boat People of Southeast Asia*. Singapore: National Museum Publication. First edition in 1965.

Straits Times (1980) 21 December. Singapore.

Suryadinata, Leo (1986) *Pribumi Indonesians, The Chinese Minority and China: A Study of Perceptions and Policies*. Singapore: Heinemann Asia.

Swettenham, Frank Athelstane (1895) *Malay Sketches*. London: John Lane.

Tanner, Adrian (1979) *Bringing Home Animals: Religious Ideology and Mode of Production of the Mistassini Cree Hunters*. London: C. Hurst and Company.

Tarling, Nicholas (1963) *Piracy and Politics in the Malay World: A Study of British Imperialism in Nineteenth-century South-east Asia*. Melbourne: F.W. Cheshire.

Tate, D.J.K. (1971) *The Making of Modern Southeast Asia. Vol. 1: The European Conquest*. Kuala Lumpur, London: Oxford University Press.

Tempo (1975) 15 February. Jakarta.

Thomas, Nicholas (1991) *Entangled Objects: Exchange, Material Culture and Colonialism in the Pacific*. Cambridge, Massachusetts: Harvard University Press.

Thomson, J.T. (1847a) 'A Glance at Rhio,' *Journal of the Indian Archipelago and Eastern Asia* 1, pp. 68-74.

– (1847b) 'Remarks on the Seletar and Sabimba Tribes,' *Journal of the Indian Archipelago and Eastern Asia* 1, pp. 341-51.

– (1851) 'Description of the Eastern Coast of Johor and Pahang, and the Adjacent Islands,' *Journal of the Indian Archipelago and Eastern Asia* 1, pp. 341-51.

Trocki, Carl A. (1979) *Prince of Pirates: The Temenggongs and the Development of Johor and Singapore 1784-1885*. Singapore: Singapore University Press.

Vos, Reinout (1993) *Gentle Janus, Merchant Prince: The VOC and the Tightrope of Diplomacy in the Malay World, 1740-1800*. Translated by Beverley Jackson. Leiden: KITLV Press.

Wang, Gungwu (1990) *The Culture of Chinese Merchants*. Working Paper Series No. 57 (March). Ontario: University of Toronto-York University, Joint Centre for Asia Pacific Studies.

Wee, Vivienne (1985) *Melayu: Hierarchies of Being in Riau*. Australian National University. Unpublished Ph.D. thesis.

– (1988) 'Material Dependence and Symbolic Independence: Constructions of Melayu Ethnicity in Island Riau, Indonesia,' in: Terry A. Rambo,

Kathleen Gillogly and Karl L. Hutterer (eds) *Ethnic Diversity and the Control of Natural Resources in Southeast Asia*. Ann Arbor: University of Michigan, Center for South and Southeast Asian Studies (Michigan Papers on South and Southeast Asia 32), pp. 197-226.

Wee, Vivienne and Cynthia Chou (1997) 'Continuity and Discontinuity in the Multiple Realities of Riau,' in: Cynthia Chou and Will Derks (eds) *Riau in Transition. Bijdragen Tot de Taal-, Land- en Volkenkunde* 153, pp. 527-41.

Wehr, Hans (1976) *A Dictionary of Modern Written Arabic*. Edited by Milton Cowan. Ithaca: Spoken Language Services.

Weiner, Annette B. (1985) 'Inalienable Wealth,' *American Ethnologist: Journal of the American Ethnological Society* 12/2, pp. 210-27.

Wilkinson, R.J. 1959. *A Malay-English Dictionary (Romanised)*. London: Macmillan.

Williams-Hunt, P.D.R. (1952) *An Introduction to the Malayan Aborigines*. Kuala Lumpur: The Government Press.

Winstedt, R.O. (1938) 'The Malay Annals on Sejarah Melayu: The Earliest Recension from MS. No. 18 of the Raffles Collection, in the Library of the Royal Asiatic Society, London,' in: *Journal of the Malayan Branch of the Royal Asiatic Society* 16/3, pp. 1-226.

– (1956) *The Malays: A Cultural History*. London/Singapore: Kelly and Walsh.

– (1961) *The Malay Magician: Being Shaman, Saiva and Sufi*. London: Routledge and Kegan Paul.

– (1979) *A History of Johor (1365-1895)*. Kuala Lumpur: The Malaysian Branch of the Royal Asiatic Society.

Wolters, O.W. (1967) *Early Indonesian Commerce*. Ithaca: Cornell University Press.

– (1970) *The Fall of Srivijaya in Malay History*. London: Asia Major Library.

Wong, Poh Kam and Ng Chee Yuen (1991) 'Singapore's Internationalization Strategy for the 1990s,' in: Sharon Siddique and Ng Chee Yuen (eds) *Southeast Asian Affairs*. Singapore: Institute for Southeast Asian Studies, pp. 267-76.

Wyllie, R.W. (1990) 'Introspective Witchcraft among the Effutu,' in: Max Marwick (ed.) *Witchcraft and Sorcery: Selected Readings*. London: Penguin Books, pp. 132-9.